THE YOUNG ADULT PLAYBOOK

The Young Adult Playbook

Living Like It Matters

ANNA B. MORELAND
AND THOMAS W. SMITH

The Catholic University of America Press
Washington D.C.

*Excluded from the copyright claim are the two poems
which are used with permission. These are:*

Dana Gioia, "The Road" from *99 Poems: New and Selected*.
Copyright © 2001 by Dana Gioia. Reprinted with the permission
of The Permissions Company, LLC on behalf of Graywolf Press,
Minneapolis, Minnesota, graywolfpress.org.

"For a New Beginning" from *To Bless the Space Between Us: A Book of Blessings*
by John O'Donohue, copyright © 2008 by John O'Donohue.
Used by permission of Doubleday, an imprint of the Knopf Doubleday Publishing Group,
a division of Penguin Random House LLC. All rights reserved.

The paper used in this publication meets the minimum requirements
of American National Standards for Information Science—
Permanence of Paper for Printed Library Materials, ANSI Z39.48-1992.

Library of Congress Cataloging-in-Publication Data
NAMES
Moreland, Anna Bonta, author. | Smith, Thomas W., 1965- author.
TITLE
The Young Adult Playbook: Living Like It Matters
Anna B. Moreland and Thomas W. Smith.
DESCRIPTION
Washington, D.C.: The Catholic University of America Press, [2024]
Includes bibliographical references.
IDENTIFIERS
LCCN 2024024578 (print) | LCCN 2024024579 (ebook)
ISBN 978-0-8132-3920-0 (paperback) | ISBN 978-0-8132-3921-7 (ebook)
SUBJECTS
LCSH: Young adults—Life skills guides.
CLASSIFICATION
LCC HQ799.5 .M665 2024 (print) | LCC HQ799.5 (ebook)
DDC 650.1084/2—dc23/eng/20240615
LC record available at https://lccn.loc.gov/2024024578
LC ebook record available at https://lccn.loc.gov/2024024579

Book design by Burt&Burt
Interior typeset in Meta Serif Pro, Epicursive Script, and Chalkboard

FOR OUR STUDENTS

Acknowledgments

This book emerged out of decades of listening to our students, in class, during office hours, in the hallways, in our homes. The stories in this book are an amalgam of their voices and hopes, their struggles and triumphs.

Students in Villanova's *Shaping a Life* curriculum read and reread different versions of the manuscript. Their feedback and encouragement helped us find our voice and strengthen this book. Students from the Collegium Institute, the Witherspoon Institute, and the Tikvah Fund also read versions of this manuscript and provided helpful comments.

Research assistants who worked on this book include: Tim Long, Franki Rudensky, Declan Carolan, Hannah Simon, Julia Paiano, and Maddie Vennerstrom. Alumni who read the whole manuscript including Keenan Lynch, Brittany Schrader, Agnes Cho, Margot Varrichio, Emily Folse, Josh Koss, Sara Lutkewitte, and Allison Porzio. We would not have been able to write this book without students sharing their stories with us. Here, we'd like to thank in particular: Rachel Constant, Gabriela Calo, Josh Koss, AJ Fezza, and Sara Lutkewitte. Audiences' feedback has proven invaluable, including at The University of Notre Dame, Chaminade University (Hawaii), The Catholic University of America, Villanova University, Loyola University of Chicago, John Carroll University, Princeton Theological Seminary, Baylor University, University of Southern California, and The Dominican School of Philosophy and Theology.

Suzanne Smith is a pediatric psychologist with twenty-five years of clinical experience. Her insights and wisdom show up everywhere.

Katherine Smith provided invaluable feedback on the final version of the manuscript. Juan Pablo, Sebastian, Margarita, and Tomas Moreland offered helpful advice along the way. Michael Moreland read numerous drafts of the manuscript and helped us with our authorial voice. Friends like Matthew Rose, Renee Massaua, and Christine Palus proved indispensable sounding boards. Our colleagues in the Humanities Department and the Honors Program at Villanova and the School of Arts and Sciences at Catholic University provided crucial encouragement throughout the drafting process. Fran Maier, Stephen Wrinn, and Bill Barry shared their wisdom about the publishing industry with us. Finally, we're grateful to the team at CUA Press, including Trevor Lipscombe and Brian Roach, for believing in our work, and to John Martino's keen editorial eye and careful stewardship.

THE ROAD

He sometimes felt that he had missed his life
    By being far too busy looking for it.
Searching the distance, he often turned to find
    That he had passed some milestone unaware,
And someone else was walking next to him,
    First friends, then lovers, now children and a wife.
They were good company–generous, kind,
    But equally bewildered to be there.

He noticed then that no one chose the way—
    All seemed to drift by some collective will.
The path grew easier with each passing day,
    Since it was worn and mostly sloped downhill.
The road ahead seemed hazy in the gloom.
    Where was it he had meant to go, and with whom?

Dana Gioia

Contents

Introduction

When Success Is a Failure

MEET JONAH

In his freshman year in college, Jonah feels like he's made it. Back in high school he did everything right. He crafted the perfect college application: all the AP classes he could take, mock trial, varsity swim team, co-captain of varsity soccer. He didn't have time for a summer job. He had to volunteer as a camp counselor to prove he was committed to service. He didn't have time for a girlfriend, either. He didn't drink (much) or smoke or do drugs. He played by all the rules—even when there seemed to be a million of them. "All the sacrifices will be worth it someday," he kept telling himself. After all, how many times did his parents say, "College is the ticket to success?" He shows up at his dream college full of hope, having spent his whole life working for this moment. A few days in, his orientation counselor tells him to sign up for as many activities as possible and then drop some later. Turns out, this was easier said than done, with emails flying in faster than raindrops during the wet monsoon season.

But by sophomore year, Jonah starts to feel stuck. From the outside, everything is going along the way it did in high school. He's a straight A student at the school of his dreams. The next steps on his path seem clear:

declare a marketable major, secure an internship, keep up with service and leadership activities, and then finally land a great job. Then he will be happy. But Jonah is starting to doubt that he'll reach the happiness he's working toward. He can't seem to choose the right major because he doesn't know what job he wants. Plus, Jonah is plagued by the feeling that the "success" at the end of this path just means more of the same: instead of working really hard in high school to get into the perfect college, now he's working really hard to land the perfect job. But, then what? Work hard at his first job to land a management position? Work extra hard in management to earn enough to retire early? When will he *truly* get to be happy?

It's not just the anxiety that he won't be happy with his eventual job. His problems run deeper than that. Jonah also wants a girlfriend and doesn't know how to get one. Even worse, he doesn't feel like he can tell his friends what he's going through. Everyone is so busy. The only plans on offer for free time involve partying and getting wasted. He used to play pickup basketball on the weekends with his friends. Now he's playing more and more Xbox alone in his room. Or watching porn on his phone.

By the beginning of his senior year, Jonah is facing a crisis. It seems impossible to hear anything beyond the songs the sirens are singing to lure him onto the rocks of toxic success. Even if he finds a different path, he'll be terrified to walk it. His parents, his teachers, his friends are all entranced by the siren songs. Jonah wants good work, but he doesn't know where to look for it. He wants a meaningful relationship but can't figure out how to get it. He's exhausted. Burnt out. He's bored with the things he does in his free time but doing anything else is too much work. Someone needs to help Jonah imagine a new future and begin to carve a path to get there.

So many readers recognize themselves in Jonah, whether they're in high school and college, or in their twenties and beyond. They work hard. They make plans. But they still feel stuck—in their work, in their free time, in their relationships.

SUPERMARKET U

College students hear a lot about the importance of landing a prestigious job. But not much about how to shape a life. They run through college like the marathon that was high school, where there was a clear finish line

2

and bright guiding markers. But there's no clear course when you get to college. College isn't a marathon. It's more like a big, confusing supermarket where students encounter thousands of bewildering options—majors, minors, credentials, study abroad programs, to say nothing of new choices about dating and alcohol and friends. But they don't know what ingredients to put in their shopping carts because they don't know what to make for dinner, and they worry that sampling different foods will waste too much time. Some throw *everything* into their carts, and then can't choose what to cook. Many don't know what they're hungry for, what good food tastes like, and how much the manic four-year shopping spree will cost in their ultimate well-being. They do know what it will cost in dollars, but that just adds to the anxiety.

Data show that life won't necessarily improve when they move into the real world. For many, the twenties are full of upheavals, dislocations, temporary jobs, aimlessness, alienation, and fear of the future. Twenty-somethings often drift through a "lost decade." Ironically, the twenties are the critical period for adult development. Clinical psychologist Meg Jay points out that twenty-something brains undergo an enormous growth spurt as they're rewired for adulthood. Female fertility peaks at age 28. The first ten years of one's working life enormously impact the trajectory of professional development over a lifetime. The twenties are not really a time for drifting; they are the time to live your life like it matters. But how?

Let's kick anxiety out of the driver's seat. This book unties the knot of success by reframing familiar stories. It illuminates fractured experiences. It offers a hopeful vision of a good life and the courage to walk a new path. It reconsiders our most important relationships—with work and free time, with friends and romantic partners. There is a playbook for genuine success—but it's not just a bunch of hoops to jump through. Rather than hurtling you into yet another marathon, this book encourages you to pause and reflect upon life's possibilities.

Our book is born from concern and hope. We are concerned about the unprecedented challenges young adults face. At the same time, we are convinced that compelling stories, sound practical advice, elevated expectations, and renewed habits make a real difference. We've seen it work so many times. We also know that there are many books written for young adults, almost as many as there are majors and minors in college.

But they're all process driven. They assume that young adults have already made decisions about the life they want, so they offer tools to help them get there, whatever the "there" is. They shy away from making claims about what makes a life worth living. Sometimes they try to provide a roadmap to "success," assuming its meaning is a given. But what sense does it make to take all the right turns if you don't know where you're going?

The Young Adult Playbook is different. We offer a map *and* a destination. So often young adults settle for surface desires, when what they ultimately want runs much deeper. The first step to your destination is understanding your deepest desires. While searching for a lucrative career, you really long for meaningful work. You feel like you can't stop "wasting time," but you really desire to have enough free time and energy to pay attention to something meaningful beyond work. Your desire for sex and romance points to a deeper desire for intimacy. As caring and effective college professors, we have spent decades guiding our students through this impoverished landscape. We can do the same for you.

Our book is organized around the places where young adults get stuck: work, free time, and romance. Each section diagnoses the struggle, offers new vocabulary, and blazes a trail to living like it matters. This doesn't mean that everyone's successful life is exactly the same—the destination is truly your own. But we have walked alongside enough of your peers that we can give you a playbook that will work for you, too. Walking this walk involves commitment and courage. But it pays off. It changes habits. It opens possibilities. It shapes a life worth living.

HOW TO READ THIS BOOK

This book is designed to connect you to your deeper hopes and dreams, to uncover who you really are and what you want out of life. Journal exercises are peppered throughout the book to help you pause and engage with the stories on a deeper level. Blank pages are included in the back if you'd like to write your responses right in the book. Take the opportunity to stop and reflect on your own choices, your own experiences. The more you engage with the exercises, the more you'll get out of this book, and the more prepared you'll be to cross that threshold into a happy, fulfilling, and generous adulthood.

After reading this book, readers make comments like this one:

I felt heard. I felt seen. I felt understood. I saw myself in the struggles of the people quoted in the book and felt comforted to know that I was not alone in my confusion throughout college and into adulthood. I wish I had had a book like this when I started college.

Throughout the chapters, you'll meet characters who are based on real people, but these are composites of several different stories, of our own stories even. You'll meet more characters like Jonah. These fictional characters are rooted in the experiences of people just like you. Listen to them.

Section 1: Work

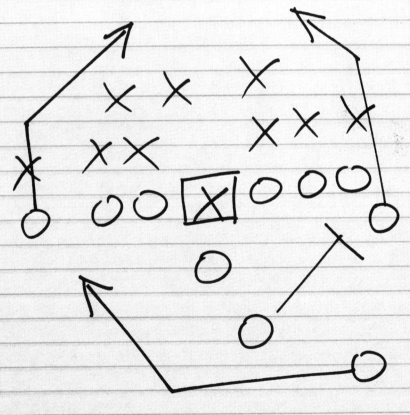

1

Stuck in Success

Like Jonah, roommates Brooke and Sofia find themselves confused about their future. Neither of their paths reflects who they are or what they really want. Both succeeded in high school and are now seniors in college. Brooke is a bright young person who looks like she's solved the job riddle. It's no wonder she's lined up a prestigious, well-paying job in New York City: she's whip smart, driven, and capable. Her roommate Sofia also survived the high school race, but she's been determined to walk away from it during college. Yet, she's flying blind.

There are those who follow the script. Those who reject it. But neither can see past it.

On the outside, Brooke is a perfect success story: she will graduate from an elite university, and has a job set up in investment banking. But here is Brooke in her own words:

> During my freshman year internship, I developed paralyzing anxiety about my future that resulted in me seeing a therapist weekly. Sophomore year, I isolated myself in my anxiety, only speaking to my boyfriend about it, losing my entire group of friends. I decided to make myself so busy that I wouldn't feel anxious. It didn't work. But it did fill my resume. I thought that would guarantee me a job and so help me deal with anxiety, but it just made things worse. Now I've got what all my friends want: a well-paying job at a top bank. But I'm not sure this is what *I* want. I feel like I backed into this career because it was something practical and prestigious.

Brooke is "succeeding" according to the measures her parents, counselors, and peers have set for her. But she hasn't figured out what success looks like *for Brooke*. After she won the high school race, she was anxious to repeat that success in college. She wanted the next medal. Freshman year, she arrived with high hopes and higher expectations. She crossed the first hurdle easily by choosing to major in finance. She had excelled in her math classes in high school and liked math. Her father had told her that finance was a versatile major. By the end of freshman year, her anxiety about choosing the right major transferred to choosing the right career. She accepted a summer internship, hoping to translate success in class into the banking industry. But on the second day of her internship, she called her parents crying after leaving work at 3:00 a.m. A taste of real working life in New York looked good on her Instagram feed, but the pressures of the banking environment were already taking a toll behind the screen. About a month into her internship, she fell apart:

> It might have been just a regular Monday in the office for most people, but for me it was the worst day of my life. I remember my hands trembling as I sat at my computer scrolling through emails, my thoughts coming so fast that my mind felt numb. I ran to the bathroom, sobbing, not knowing why I was feeling like my mind was a black hole. I called my Dad to tell him that he needed to get to New York City. Fast. He met me for lunch and I'll never forget it. I told him I couldn't live this way anymore. I never thought my life would come to this. I'm only 19.

She survived her internship and by senior year received a full-time offer. But given her internship, she harbors serious doubts. Her first investment—in her education—will produce a high monetary return. The night she accepts the offer she writes in her journal, "I want to change my life right now, but I feel stuck."

Brooke remarks, "I let my fear of failure motivate everything I do. I'm not worried about life after graduation; I'm worried about failure after graduation." She sees work through a hyper-competitive lens. She has thrown her hopes into the trunk, while her anxieties are steering in the driver's seat. In her journal, Brooke writes, "So here I am, hiding behind a shield of financial security, thinking that this will give me the freedom to do whatever

I want . . . *someday*." But will that *someday* ever come? She feels paralyzed by a desire to change but doesn't know *how* to change.

While Brooke spills her worries to her roommate Sofia about whether to accept a lucrative job offer in Manhattan, Sofia tries to listen attentively, but can't help thinking, "I wish I had your problems," followed quickly by the comforting yet judgy, "at least I'm not selling my soul for money."

Sofia took an opposite approach than her roommate in college. She arrived at campus knowing that she wanted something different from the treadmill that was high school:

> I was burned out by the time I arrived at college. I wasn't gonna do *that* again. I was done with trying to do impressive stuff. I knew there was something more. There weren't going to be the same checkmarks in college like there were in my high school. This was freeing, but it also made my freshman year full of confusion and loneliness.

In high school, Sofia felt like she was part of a team of Olympic swimmers who were trained to win the race. But to do that, they had to shave every hair on their heads and bodies. Everything that made them unique had to be stripped so they could swim faster than everyone else. This process of stripping and conforming to the rules had left her empty.

She was determined not to let this happen again by taking classes that she loved and choosing a major that was meaningful for her. Yet she had to admit that she was crippled by the fact that she hadn't filled out the checkboxes. She took courses in architectural history and the economics of poverty. Both were fascinating. Neither led to a career path. She walked out of her advisor's office during junior year in a full-blown panic. She had set up the meeting to get help about whether to work toward a history minor or double down on her English major. He started asking her questions about why she wants to minor in history. Then about why she's majoring in English. Then he asked her about her plans after graduation. She walked out of there on the verge of tears.

Senior year came too quickly. Sofia didn't have a job. What's worse, she had *no idea* what she wanted to do with her life. Her liberal arts classes, while fulfilling, hadn't led to any magical solutions to her career dilemma. Sofia would later reflect back upon her anxieties of senior year:

I found myself thinking about career paths because I was so concerned with what I would tell my family and friends when they asked what I was going to do, rather than really listening to myself. When I graduated college and wasn't yet sure of next steps, I was so anxious that I literally rehearsed an answer to the dreaded question of "What's next?" I did have possible plans, but I was worried about how they'd be perceived.

Choices are risky. Scary. In her book, *The Defining Decade*, Meg Jay talks about a powerful swimmer stuck out in the middle of the ocean. She's got the skills to swim anywhere. But she can't decide where to go so she treads water in the same place. She obsesses over her options, tries to listen to every voice in her head, and weighs every possible decision against the others. Sofia feels like this swimmer.

The problem for both Brooke and Sofia is that the current collegiate environment—regardless of what major students pursue—doesn't help them expand their imaginations about meaningful work. The two options on the table are being too practical and not being practical enough. Brooke majors in Finance. Sofia majors in English. But by senior year, neither has developed an effective vocabulary about meaningful work. Brooke, Sofia, and students like them find themselves trapped, either heading for a job they worry will destroy them or heading for no job at all and having no idea how to find a fulfilling one.

This chapter invites you to move to a deeper level when talking about work—the level that really matters. Young adults are told that they have to find work, but nobody talks about what work is, the place it occupies in a good life, and how to find good work. In order to figure out the one pressing question—what should I do for a living?—you have to get deeper into the meaning of work and how it fits into your life as a whole. These involve underlying issues about identity: Who am I? Who do I want to become through my work? What are my gifts? How can these gifts make the world a better place? This chapter will offer new vocabulary to expand your imagination about future jobs, challenging what "success" in work actually means. The next chapter will arm you with practical tools to make decisions about work that *actually work*.

THE SORT

What has the relentless drive for productivity done to Brooke and Sofia? It has sorted them. Our educational culture resembles the Sorting Ceremony in *Harry Potter*, where students at Hogwarts are sorted into one of four houses by placing a magical hat on their heads that declares which house a student will join. The sorting is qualitative: each house reflects the talents and personalities of the students who live in them and prepares them for their future in the wizarding world. The students facing the Sorting Ceremony are nervous. It decides their fate. In *Harry Potter*, the sorting hat tries to figure out what's best for you, and there is no chance for appeal. With Harry Potter himself, the hat sees two possible paths and asks what he wants, but this seems to be rare. We are not in the wizarding world, and students in our schools are said to choose their own path. But in reality, the current system of preparation for work resembles a lifelong Sorting Ceremony in which young adults are slotted into careers they didn't actually choose.

College students sometimes feel like their whole lives have been one long sort. They're measured all the time: through standardized tests, GPA, or extracurricular activities and accomplishments. For high schoolers, college admissions committees are the real "sorting hat." In fact, the competition to get into the "best" colleges gets more challenging every year. A few decades ago, the most competitive colleges accepted a much larger percentage of their applicants than now. For example, in 2005, the University of Chicago accepted forty percent of applicants. Now it accepts around five percent.

Success in the sorting process means clearing a *succession* of well-defined hurdles. The first hurdle is getting into a good college. Colleges teach you to build brands that you can sell on the market to get that good job. You need "brand proof points": diplomas from elite universities, prestigious internships, distinctive study abroad experiences, and the right activities. Most of you are so busy navigating the sorting process that you have no time for deeper questions.

Every new sorting process is one that somebody else has set. You arrive at college burdened with the expectations of others on your shoulders, primarily the expectations of your parents, but also those of your wider circles of family and friends. And college admissions committees you'll never see. *But when do you get to discover the path that makes the most sense for you—the unique person the earth has never seen before and will never see again, who has her own desires, his own talents, and their own hopes?*

THE GIFT

The first step in finding good work is to expand your imagination. To widen your sense of the scope of meaningful work, we'll turn to an unexpected source: the creation story in the *Book of Genesis*. We're going to talk about this story in a way no one else does: as a way to explore the meaning of work. In *Genesis*, work has meaning. But it serves a larger purpose—a life well-lived.

In the story, God works; he creates light, darkness, and all the living things on the earth. He makes humans in his image and tells them to be fruitful and multiply. Then God rests and calls creation—his work—good. The story then zooms in from the creation of the whole world to the first human beings. God creates Adam and Eve, and he invites them to participate in his creative work by cultivating the Garden of Eden. This work ennobles them. The garden beautifies nature and feeds the creatures in it. Work is valuable because it serves and signifies. It serves by providing things like sustenance and shelter. It signifies by pointing from creation to its creator. These gardeners plant and plow. But the seeds and soil, the water and sun, existed before their work began. Adam and Eve's work is an important but limited part of the overall organism. Their work is a gift within a much larger horizon of the gift of being alive.

As the story starts, Adam and Eve are like little children, and their work is like play. They don't know they are naked and vulnerable. And just like very young children, they don't know they're going to die. But then they grow up. In eating the apple that the serpent offers them, Adam and Eve are shocked into the realities of vulnerability and death. They point fingers and blame each other for their problems; and they start to think of each other as competitors. Work moves from being understood as a gift to becoming a burden involving toil and strife.

The work that Adam and Eve had been given to do in the garden initially was a privilege. At the end of the story, they still have a job to do, and it still involves working with the earth. But now their work brings frustration and worry. In forgetting the giftedness of work, Adam and Eve seek to control and bend it to their own purposes. It becomes something they have to dominate to make their lives feel more secure. This attitude of control and risk minimization is at the heart of the difficulties with work. In the *Genesis* story, work is built into the human DNA. It is fundamental to the meaning of existence. Meaningful work is one of the keys to our happiness. For this reason, we are tempted to overvalue work, placing it at the center of our lives. But overvaluing it makes us lose sense of its real value. The paradox is that once work is reduced *solely* to securing a living, it actually becomes more difficult. Once we make work *only* about securing the instrumental goods we need for life, it loses meaning.

This story reveals something important about the human relationship to work. Work is about securing the conditions for our lives, to be sure. Everyone has to figure out a way to make a living. But finding meaningful work is part of our human task too. We can find creative ways of making work more human, more thoughtful, more intentional. Good work is at the heart of who we are. It's ultimately a gift that develops our natural capacities to cultivate the world. When we do good work, we enjoy our work, we find delight in it, and we become more human in the process.

Brooke and Sofia need to find work that brings them out of themselves, cultivates the garden around them, and makes them more human. It is hard for Brooke to see beyond the prestige of the banking industry. But there's another option besides gritting her teeth and getting through each day or running away from the stress and anxiety. Instead, she should think about how her work serves the people around her. This job will build her banking expertise. To what end? Who will her clients be? Maybe Brooke was born to be a banker. But what kind of banker? Serving what kind of people and what kind of community? Brooke needs to set aside what she thinks she wants—prestige, wealth, security—and think instead about whom and what her work could serve. She needs to consider work in both its dimensions: it's not only a way to make a living, but also a path to meaning.

Even though Sofia the English major has taken a different approach to college, as she tries to find a way to turn her education into employment, she should ask herself the same questions. She has treated college like a supermarket that offers lots of free samples, and she is good at tasting, but all that tasting has led her nowhere. What part of the fractured world does she want to heal? And how could the ingredients she has casually tossed in her shopping cart make up a nourishing meal? That is, how can the skills and experiences she has happened to acquire add up to a way to do something useful for others? This isn't something that has to be figured out right away, as the next chapter will make clear, but until Sofia started asking herself these questions, she would have no real direction.

Journal Exercise #1
- Imagine your dream job.
- Set aside practical considerations.
- Think big here.
- Jot ideas as they occur to you.
- Remember what you wanted to do for a living when you were a child.
- Write down multiple jobs.
- Don't write in full sentences.

Even while being fed false stories about the sorting process, you know that your personal identity is bound up with the work you'll do. *Who you are* relates to the career you will occupy: your social and economic status, the meaning of your life, and your own sense of self. Work is an important dimension of a life well-lived. But it needs to be placed in a wider frame than just wealth and prestige. Through work you will discover one of the ways to find your *true purpose* in the world. But a lot of people get stuck translating this innate sense into practical reality.

Work confers an important dimension of personal identity. But loading work with *all* of our personal identity is too heavy a burden for it to bear. If we think work confers ultimate meaning, identity, and purpose, it would be hard for us to place necessary limits to protect life outside of work. Work has to be bounded, limited by something it serves. Unbounded work threatens to take over everything. It squeezes out the time needed to build a family, make good friends, and engage in meaningful activities. All-consuming work can threaten the good things it's meant to serve. So, work needs guardrails.

Focus on what work serves and place limits on its demands.

The gift of work—the job given to each one of you—takes on meaning insofar as it enters into a relationship with goods that go beyond the work and the worker. Like good love, good work is ecstatic; that is, it takes you out of your self-focus, but in a way that leaves you feeling fulfilled. Meaningful work serves the world and the people in it. That is the job you're called to do. And your work will be meaningful to the extent to which you get caught up in a creative devotion to what your work serves. A good doctor cares for the health of her patients. That is what her work serves. A doctor is called "good" as she develops all the skills involved in fostering the health of the people under her care. If she only cares about her status as a surgeon or the money she makes, she might be competent, but she's not fully a good doctor. A good carpenter cares about the cabinet he is making. He will get paid for his work, but while he's working, he's not thinking about the money. He's thinking about the cabinet. In a sense, his work serves the cabinet that is being produced and the home where it will be placed.

With this renewed sense of the importance and limits of work, we need a different way of imagining work, one in which *work confers personal meaning, but only as it is oriented toward a life well-lived*. This approach must be practical, but there are no simple instructions here. "Skills of discernment" will help you understand what kind of work makes sense *for you*. You will develop these skills to discover your own path. Let's reorient the question from "what job will be a return on your investment in education"—the normal way to think about work—and towards "what job will make you a better person and enable you to serve the community in which you live?" When our English major Sofia writes in her journal about this question, she finds herself remembering her experiences as a summer camp counselor. She *loved* helping homesick kids overcome their anxieties and plug into the camp activities. She wishes she could be a camp counselor for life.

Untying the work knot means both *elevating* and *limiting* work. Ultimately, deciding your career path will certainly include practical considerations—like salary and place of work and advancement opportunity—but the answer will not be reduced to just these considerations. Meaningful work not only makes the worker a better person, but it also improves the community —social, political, or economic—around us. Work needs to find its proper place in life, not overvaluing it but not undervaluing it either. A new approach and a new vocabulary will open your imagination to possibilities that seem closed in our current culture. *Work confers personal meaning, but only as it is oriented towards a life well-lived*.

2

Work That Works for You

How often do you think about your future? Current research in psychology suggests that thinking about the future is vital to several key areas of life. It can influence whether you choose a smaller reward now or a larger one in the future. Thinking about your future gives you a distanced perspective, helping you move through complicated issues in a more successful way. Finally, it can help you make better, more sound decisions.

This chapter is about training you to move through decisions about work wisely. Below, we'll walk you through five steps on the path to finding good work that's right for you. First, you do the prep work that opens up your imagination (Step One). Then, you identify the crossroads in your professional life (Step Two) and gather the necessary resources (Step Three) to make a choice (Step Four). Finally, it's important to check in with those you trust as a way of confirming the path you should take (Step Five).

STEPS TOWARDS FINDING GOOD WORK

Step One: Breaking the Frame

Many students assume that if they just think long and hard about a problem, they'll work their way through it. Young adults tend put a lot of stock in their mental calculations. But this strategy often ignores the imagination. A lot of time is spent agonizing over what to do, even just what to do next. This question of the future seems to be just one big, confounding puzzle. The reality is that the question of the future—both professionally and personally—is a whole series of puzzles that can't just be solved in your head, and there will be a few unexpected turns along the way.

Young adults struggle to come up a wide array of career prospects. How did this happen? Canadian philosopher Charles Taylor suggests that a community shapes its inhabitants' imaginations in ways that are often difficult to grasp. He calls this the "social imaginary." Taylor's "social imaginary" is not a set of clear ideas learned in a course or training, but a somewhat elusive set of self-understandings, background practices, and horizons of common expectations. These are often expressed in images or stories, imparting a shared sense of what's "normal" or even possible. The social imaginary isn't easily captured. Getting people to understand the social imaginary is more like getting fish to notice they are swimming in water.

Try to see the social imaginary that's affecting you around work. Do you notice that only a few disciplines seem "worthy" when you're asked, "what's your major?" The social imaginary restricts the way you think about choosing a major or searching for a job. Has society pushed jobs outside your field of vision that don't conform to the well-worn paths of business, medicine, or law? Or within the community you grew up in, are construction or farming the expected occupations?

Ask yourself: what are the horizons and expectations that come to mind when you ask the question, "What do I want to do with my life?" Do they make you less creative than you could be about your plans for the future? In other words, the social imaginary can make you believe that there are only a few "practical" occupations worth pursuing. Brooke's parents, for example, always steered her toward lucrative career options, jobs where she could "make good money." Sofia's parents, by contrast, urged her towards STEM fields that will always be in demand—her father was a computer programmer, and her mother a nurse. Unlike Brooke, though, Sofia rebelled against those expectations and became an English major, which left her unqualified for a STEM career. But because of her social imaginary, she was then unable to foresee what kinds of jobs she might do with her skills and abilities.

Some, of course, genuinely love finance or want to become doctors or attorneys. That's terrific. Maybe you are one of them. But not everyone is. If we're going to find work that works for each of us, we need to widen the panoply of possible jobs, to look beyond the horizon of our social imaginary. We need a playbook that has more pages.

The good life includes a lot of good things. But "the sorting ceremony" that happens in our schools (see chapter 1) focuses only on narrowly defined "success." That's not good for us as individuals, and it's not good for our society. Here's what New York Times columnist David Brooks says about it:

> As a sorting divide [the modern meritocracy machine] is batshit crazy. The ability to perform academic tasks during adolescence is nice to have, but organizing your society around it is absurd. That ability is not as important as the ability to work in teams; to sacrifice for the common good; to be honest, kind, and trustworthy; to be creative and self-motivated. A sensible society would reward such traits by conferring status on them. A sensible society would not celebrate the skills of a corporate consultant while slighting the skills of a home nurse.

Our society needs more than just consultants. Have you ever met a beekeeper or a cartoonist? Have you ever asked yourself what it takes to become a landscape architect or what a career in urban planning might look like? Have you ever wondered who chose the plants in the city's arboretum? Or who has the job that plans better electrical grids to power those telephone lines that go down during storms? What about all the jobs surrounding law enforcement or the military?

Journal Exercise #2

Go to your journal and let your mind wander. Think about people who work in your local community. What kinds of jobs come into your imagination? What people do you know who seem to love what they do? Why do you think they enjoy their work so much? Create as long a list as you can.

If you are having trouble creating a list, that tells you something about your social imaginary. If you can't stop writing possible occupations, you're priming the pump for your own career discernment.

If not, it's because your imaginations have been narrowed by the social imaginary that sees work primarily *as a return on an investment*. You may think that the only purpose of work is to make money, cultivate prestige, and obtain status. What else could work be, you may ask. Novelist Dorothy Sayers expresses our perspective well: work should be understood, "not as a necessary drudgery to be undergone for the purpose of making money, but as a way of life in which the nature of [the human person] should find its proper exercise and delight."

Choosing meaningful work allows you to develop your talents.

The question isn't only "What am I good at?" but also "What do I want to *become* good at?" Meaningful work makes you more of who you are. As you learn, you grow and develop, you become more human. You have to start somewhere, or else you'll never become good at anything. In short, you should work as Sayers reminds us "for the sake of doing well a thing that is well worth doing."

Why should you consign work to the task of just making money? Who wants to go to a doctor who's just in it for the money and prestige and doesn't care about whether his patient gets better? Who would trust a lawyer who badmouths her clients and their problems behind their backs and sees her job as a way of personal advancement? Why would you want to learn to play a sport from a coach who is just trying to supplement his teaching salary and doesn't love the game?

Networking Exercise
Find two people who have jobs outside your own field of vision. Set up a call, a Zoom appointment, or an in-person meeting with these people and ask them how they got into their line of work. You might not find the person who points you to "your" job, but you'll start to expand your social imaginary around work.

Looking for meaningful work could mean that you become someone in a traditional "helping" profession—a nurse, a teacher, a therapist, a librarian—but that's not the only meaningful path. It could mean that you build something or make something worthwhile—a cabinetmaker, a chef, an architect, a brewmaster. It could just mean that you become a shoe salesperson who actually cares about fitting shoes to people's feet, or an accountant who enjoys working with numbers and strives to be honest, or a government regulator who implements laws to help people. Because the field is so wide open, in fact, it can be hard to know what to do next.

Step Two: Recognizing the Crossroads

Let's return to Sofia's story. Soon after graduation, she reaches out to a family friend who runs a small tech startup. Sofia has always admired this friend of her father's. As it happens, one of the administrative assistants at the firm is going on parental leave for three months. This gives Sofia the perfect opportunity to earn a paycheck while trying to figure out what she wants to do with her life. And she knows this job is temporary, so it buys her some time to send out applications. She has rid herself of the illusion of finding that perfect first job that unites work and identity. And yet, she builds unexpected identity capital during this job. Identity capital is the sum of individual choices and experiences that she collects over time that makes her who she is. She is learning that she has administrative skills and that she's good at negotiating conflict. She has taken the first practical step after graduation to earn a living while she figures out her next step. She is ready to attack an important puzzle: is she going to get another job or apply to graduate school? If she applies to graduate school, what master's program does she want to pursue?

Many young people who want meaningful work don't find the next step so easily. When facing career decisions, students are often trapped into thinking that they have to find *the one job that will fulfill all their expectations*. But the unfolding of a career path so often doesn't happen that way. The path to real success is not a straight line. It is full of twists and turns and unexpected breakthroughs or road bumps. There are moments along the way, though, when you will face a fork in the road, where option A beckons you down one road, and option B toward another.

Joseph Badaracco, professor at Harvard Business School, offers a practical framework to work through these decisions in his book *Defining Moments*. He insists that, in almost all cases, one path isn't "good" and the other "evil." Instead, you'll have to decide between the "good" path and the "better" path, whether it's a choice of jobs, internship opportunities, or majors. Instead of worrying about making a mistake, think about how this decision will reveal who you are, test your character, and shape your future.

When facing a defining moment, it's often helpful to list the goods that each option brings with it. Often, the goods of one option are in tension with the goods in the other option. Thinking of your list in terms of "goods in play" rather than "pro/con" will help you move to deeper levels of concerns and commitments. Reframing your defining moment will free you from the "right" vs. "wrong" mindset. You'll weigh goods in relation to your whole life, and you'll realize that deciding in favor of one set of goods often brings with it leaving behind another set of goods. Life is just "tragic" that way; to have anything, you have to give up something else. For Brooke and so many like her, anxiety often sits in the driver's seat during defining moments, focusing all the attention on what will be lost, and obscuring what can be gained. In what follows, we'll provide exercises to help you kick that anxiety to the curb.

Moments of career decision certainly help define your character. They cast a shadow forward into your future. And yet as your professional life unfolds, so will these moments. It's very unusual for you to make a decision or commitment that you can't undo later on in your professional life. It's not necessary to think each decision is "all or nothing." The key to overcoming anxiety is retraining your imagination.

Journal Exercise #3

Think of a defining moment you've been through or are going through. You're stuck between option "A" and option "B." Write down what "goods are in play" on either side of the decision. This isn't a typical "pro vs. con" list, as you're identifying "pros" on either side of your decision. Reframing your decision in terms of possibilities rather than drawbacks can sometimes open things up.

Set aside your anxiety. Examine the goods you've written down, note how they are in tension, but weigh the one set of goods against the other. No need to come to a decision. This is an exercise in weighing the goods that are in play in this decision.

Step Three: Identifying Resources

Because of the "social imaginary," you have to use your imagination to actively train your brain to think outside the box. To see work possibilities beyond the mainstream, take note of people and occupations that you normally let fade to the background. So seek out concrete images. You need to ask yourself, "Who do I want to become?" through a comparison with people that you can respect or admire.

The woman Sofia had replaced for parental leave chose not to come back to the tech startup. When Sofia was offered a full-time position, she decided to accept because she still needed more time to figure out whether or not to go to graduate school, and even if she decided to go, she was having trouble deciding whether to choose an MFA or to study journalism. It had been eighteen months since Sofia decided to stay in that company, and she was still feeling pulled in two directions. One night as she was walking home from work, she was scrolling on social media and saw that modern American novelist and essayist Marilynne Robinson was going to speak at the Folger Library in nearby Washington, DC, about one of her books that had just been published. Sofia decided to attend the event the next day.

As she listened to how articulate, composed, smart, and insightful Marilynne Robinson was, she thought to herself, "I want to be like *her*." Robinson mentioned that after she threw out her TV, she felt as though her life became seven times as long. The author didn't blink at telling people about this radical move, and she was comfortable in her own skin. There was just an unapologetic presence to her. It was a pivotal moment in Sofia's life, and it played an important role in her decision to go to graduate school to pursue an MFA. That night in the Folger Library, Sofia realized something was missing from her life. She wanted to study writing.

She didn't end up becoming a fiction writer like Marilynne Robinson, but she did decide to use her own interests to become her own sort of writer at an advertising agency. Finding concrete models is crucial, but this does not mean that you have to imitate that model in every respect. It is important to reflect upon what, exactly, about that model that you want to emulate, and how that fits your particular gifts, abilities, and hopes.

You might find yourself pulled toward more traditional career paths because they are well-trodden and predictable. You've been trained to plan your life in such a rigid academic structure, both in terms of timeline and the content of your time spent, that it's hard to suddenly switch your picture of the way a job or even a life goes. So many students jump toward a familiar path in the "next chapter" of their lives because that is the only language they speak, and it can be hard to break free.

Journal Exercise #4

Go to your journal. Think about three people you've met whom you admire.
- What is it about that person you admire?
- What job does that person do for a living?
- Do you look up to them? Why?

Write down the nitty gritty details about why you admire each of these people.
- What can you do to become more like them?

For instance, Xavier was planning to go to law school like many of his friends, although he didn't particularly relish the thought of being a lawyer. He was the first member of his family to attend an elite college, and they expected him to become the first to get a doctorate of some sort. His senior year, he took a philosophy of law course, and enjoyed it so much that he quickly signed up for another course with the same professor. Xavier's imagination was ignited by his philosophy professor like Sofia was ignited that night by Marilynne Robinson, but he thought that the only way to pursue this new interest and meet everyone's expectations was to get a Ph.D. in philosophy.

The problem was that, several years into graduate school, he had come to hate the isolation and pressure of writing papers. He knew the job market for his field was lousy. One day, his department held a panel for "non-traditional jobs" for philosophy graduates. There was a digital content creator, a motivational speaker, and a journals editor. Xavier couldn't imagine himself doing either of the first two, but what the editor said intrigued him. When he saw a notice for a part-time job posting at a publishing company, he quickly applied. That application led him to a full-time job and ultimately, a rewarding career.

Career panels, family friends, or chance encounters are all ways to expand your horizon, but they are not the only ways. Here, online research really helps. Find people who have the sorts of jobs you're interested in and read about their backgrounds, about how they got to where they got. Or look into graduate programs in the fields you're considering and click on the "what our graduates are doing now" link to see what jobs those students land.

To further emphasize what a huge role the imagination plays in decisions about majors and jobs, let's turn to a man named Garrison Keillor. Keillor tells a story of when he first went to the famous Grand Ole Opry in

Nashville, Tennessee as a 32-year-old man. His day job was as a radio host in Minnesota, but he was travelling to write a magazine piece about that famous theater. He had been having a hard time getting his assignments done on time for this magazine and wasn't sure what he would write. But as he sat in the balcony, what he saw made him forget his troubles:

> It was too glorious, too exotic. The pulsation of fans, people fanning themselves in this auditorium, those church windows in the back, the colors of the sequins, and the way the performers did their hair, the way the announcer gestured to the audience for applause, the crowd milling around in the wings, those pin rails along the wings with the ropes that tied to them going on up to the fly gallery. All those performers coming on with their gorgeous mother of pearl guitars and the smell of hot dogs and beer and the smell of people. All of that gaiety and confusion . . . And I thought to myself, 'You know that looks like fun down there on stage, what they're doing. Singing and entertaining these wonderful people. Wouldn't that be a great way to spend your time.'

Something about that evening, about the performers down there on stage, lit him from within. His imagination was ignited. He went home and started a Saturday night comedy radio show in a theater with music and a live audience.

If this doesn't sound like a recipe for success and stardom in 2024, it didn't in the 1970s either. Nevertheless, that risk paid off. "A Prairie Home Companion" became a national hit that ran for decades, and Keillor's voice an icon of American culture. He has written over a dozen adult and children's books and done voiceover work for Disney, Honda, and Ken Burns political documentaries. He still had a podcast at age 81. But if he hadn't taken that assignment with that magazine, if he hadn't gone to Nashville to write that piece, his imagination might never have been ignited enough to take that professional risk.

The role of the imagination is crucial in making these life decisions. But how do you choose between helpful and harmful images? How do you judge between them? Which "voices" in your head and those around you should you listen to? How do you not overly obsess about all the possible choices, leading to choice paralysis? To answer these questions, we're going to draw on another resource.

Step Four: Making a Choice

You may have heard of the Jesuits, or of Jesuit schools like Georgetown or Boston College. The Jesuits are a Catholic religious order founded by a man with a particular genius for the imagination. Ignatius of Loyola was a sixteenth century Spanish knight who suffered a war wound and spent a lot of time in a sickbed recovering from his shattered leg. He liked to read chivalric romances, but the house where he was laid up didn't have any of these. Instead, he read the only books available: about the life of Jesus of Nazareth and a book of the lives of saints.

He also spent countless hours in bed letting his imagination wander. At times, he'd imagine himself the well-mannered knight, wooing young women with his sharp wit and humor. At others, he'd imagine himself as Saint Francis of Assisi, giving all his possessions to the poor. He began to notice that he felt differently after having imagined his future life as a knight than after having imagined his future as a monk. While the imaginative moments were pleasant for both, he realized that the first left him feeling dry and dissatisfied, while after the second he felt the opposite—he felt happy, full of hope.

When he recovered, unsurprisingly, Ignatius chose the religious path, where he became a hugely successful leader of other men. More importantly for our purposes, he kept refining his processes for judging between different images of the future, which he called "discernment of spirits." These Ignatian-inspired "exercises" are part of our playbook.

For Ignatius, the first step in the discernment process involves cultivating a "detachment" to the options. This doesn't mean "I don't care what job I get." Instead, it involves developing a greater awareness of our attachments to things. When Brooke imagines her life as an investment banker, is she attracted to that life because she values what she'll accomplish through the work? Or is she attached to the wealth and prestige that comes with the position? How do the different options genuinely make her feel—trapped, anxious, afraid, or free, happy, full of hope? This is a hard yet essential thing to sort out. Developing a "detachment" to the options lying ahead helps you become more objective in your decision-making process.

Here is an example. When the possibility of Natalie's spouse leaving the financial security of law firm life and accepting a position in politics in another city became a real one, she was terrified. It was not as though the move would push their family into poverty, but it would not let them live the lifestyle to which Natalie was accustomed. That attachment to the creature comforts of a lucrative income was something to examine and discipline herself away from. Natalie had to become "detached" to the financial security of her husband's law firm. Once financial anxieties faded into the background, other advantages of moving to another city that she had been ignoring came to the foreground. The cost of living was cheaper. She would live closer to her sister. Her husband would finally have time to make dinner for the family. It's like something within her unlocked, and she was able to imagine all the advantages of a future life she hadn't anticipated. The discernment process begins by *cultivating detachment*.

Ultimately, cultivating detachment is about trying to figure out what kind of work will genuinely make you happy over a lifetime, rather than being stuck on what you have now and can't imagine your life without.

Ignatius encourages us to leap imaginatively into what option "A" looks like. Sit with an image of yourself in option "A" at age 25, 30, 55. Do that exercise repeatedly and then pay attention to how you feel after those images have retreated into the background of your mind. Ask yourself, "Do I feel consolation or desolation? Do I feel a lasting sort of peace, contentment, happiness even, or do I feel a little gross or confused?" It might be that the imaginative exercise for option "A" is initially exciting and attractive, but it is crucial

Journal Exercise #5
Go to your journal and write about your fears concerning your search for work. Often, we need to cultivate detachment around our fears in order to see more clearly. Our goal is to put our fears in the trunk so that we can let our hopes into the driver's seat. Dig deep here. Be honest with yourself.

to recognize how you feel later in the day or week when thinking back to option "A." It is important to do this exercise repeatedly and pay attention to its aftereffects. Some options that are initially attractive aren't lastingly so.

When Brooke reached her senior year, she was a typical student stuck in choice paralysis. Perhaps this is why she decided to take a course on "Shaping an Adult Life" (the basis of this book). In response to one of the journaling exercises, she wrote:

For big, life-altering decisions, I tend to be very indecisive and have trouble committing to one option. I didn't agree to start dating my high school boyfriend until the morning of prom where I knew everyone would be inquiring about our relationship status. I didn't put my college deposit down until 11:55 p.m. on May 1st because I was torn between two schools. I didn't sign my return offer until the last day of eligibility. I view making these impactful life decisions with an air of finality and I feel more comfortable when there are doors still open.

As graduation approached, following these Ignatian discernment exercises from the class, she began cultivating detachment. She imagined herself telling her family and friends about her job in investment banking and felt proud. When she thought about the cool apartment she would be able to rent in Manhattan or how people would react to her job, she became excited. But that feeling didn't last. She'd wake up the next day feeling anxious about the toll the long hours would take on her mental health. As she imagined herself in the day-to-day reality of the job itself, that pride turned into anxiety and emptiness. Her fellow interns at the bank were also stressed out. Plus, they were competitive, and they didn't talk about their lives outside the office. She realized that her excitement about the job was fleeting, and it had to do with the trappings of the job, not the job itself. Her anxiety, however, was more real and lasting.

By cultivating "detachment" toward the financial security of the job, Brooke was able to face some serious facts. While some aspects of the work itself attracted her, the demands it placed on her time, energy, and well-being left her feeling worn out. And she realized that she had let her family, her teachers, and her peers define what "success" meant to her. Cultivating detachment for Brooke required self-awareness and reflection. She used to operate under the paradigm of "deciding," where she wrote pro-con lists, and thought her head was guiding her decision. Once she gave her imagination a chance, she realized that discerning rather than deciding led her to see how blind she had been to her hunger for prestige and to her own insecurities. She was willing to look for another way.

Step Five: Checking In

The playbook for discernment does not stop at internal exercises. The next phase along the way for Ignatius involves talking to others you trust.

It's really important to lean on the guidance of these figures in your lives. This doesn't mean that you have to do what someone says because they are your parent or your close friend. You have to look for those who are more interested in your real happiness than the trappings of success. We know from experience that it can be difficult to talk to your own parents about a course correction, especially if you're afraid that it will disappoint them. You need real friends who will help you sort out which options are sound, and which are deceptively attractive. It is a good idea to choose wisely whom you want to approach. Choose figures you admire. Perhaps a family friend. Perhaps a boss from a summer job. Maybe even a neighbor. Those you approach for advice might even have concrete ideas about possible internships or first jobs.

There is one group that students often overlook, but who can be quite helpful: their teachers or professors. Often students are shy about approaching faculty members about life decisions. Those who overcome this shyness, however, are often gratified to see that their instructors care about them as individuals. More than likely, the faculty member has noticed aspects about the student or his work that help inform his decision. And if the first professor you approach is unwilling or ill-equipped to help, knock on the next one's door. Even if you have left high school or college a while ago, a favorite teacher will often be delighted to hear from you and willing to make time for you.

As Brooke was nearing graduation, she had realized that she wasn't ready to take that investment banking job. She was worried about what it would do to her mental health, especially after how hard she had worked for four years in college. But she didn't know what to do instead, or how to break her change of heart to her family. Encouraged by the class, she contacted a favorite faculty member to meet during office hours. Brooke laid out all her anxieties to her professor. After listening to her concerns, her professor responded, "Brooke, it sounds to me that at least you aren't ready to take this job right now. Have you ever thought about taking a gap year?" Brooke's first response was, "That's too risky. My family and friends will think I'm crazy." After a brief pause, her professor quietly asked, "Isn't it better to be crazy than miserable?"

Knock on the doors of adults you respect. Ask them for advice. Meg Jay talks about cultivating "weak ties" in her book *The Defining Decade*. Weak ties are those relationships you have that are outside of your inner circle of friends and family. Remember how Sofia had the courage to reach out to that family friend who ran a startup. Often the first job will come from someone who isn't in your inner circle, but with whom you've met in some way or another. Sometimes a job comes from a random contact. Sofia's current advertising job materialized as the result of a phone call from a friend of a friend from graduate school whom she had met exactly once and who wasn't even in her field of study. The strength of weak ties continues throughout your professional life. Strengthen those weak ties by contacting adults you admire and asking them for guidance.

Journal Exercise #6

Go to your journal and write a list of adults you'd like to contact about possible jobs. Or at least you want to contact them to find out how they got to their current line of work.

Don't be afraid to think big. Industry leaders, thought influencers, or folks with demanding jobs might not get back to you. But they might.

You'd be surprised at how eager people are to mentor young people who approach them with interest. Once you have a list, write up some questions that you'd like to ask.

One thing that these mentor figures will tell you is that the path is just different for different people. This discernment process comes in many shapes and sizes. It's important to pay attention to the one that makes sense for you. While most people face certain key moments in life where they choose to walk down one road rather than another, and some even have "lightning bolt" moments, for others, there emerges a slow realization over—probably—years that the professional choice made long ago actually fits.

Or that it doesn't. It was agonizing for our would-be philosopher Xavier to let go of the dream of getting the letters "PhD" after his name, and the prestige of being called "Doctor." But he realized that he no longer wanted the doctorate for the work itself—writing papers, presenting at conferences, teaching students. Instead, the work he enjoyed was in the editorial office. Once he told his dissertation director that he was discontinuing the PhD, he felt unexpectedly liberated. Within a few years, he took a promotion that allowed him to publish many of the philosophers whose work he had studied in graduate school. He only wishes that he had quit the program sooner, both for the debt he still carries and the time he lost from other pursuits.

CARVING YOUR PATH

The decisions about your major and what to do after college are important. But looking back, you'll find that these are two in a string of important life decisions during adult life. College seniors only have to decide the next step, not the next five steps. Just the next step. When Brooke decided not to take that job in Manhattan in investment banking and instead move to Brazil for a year after college, she didn't know how formative it would be. She just wasn't ready to make a big career decision. She went to live with an aunt and uncle in São Paulo and took care of their kids in exchange for room and board. Only in retrospect did she recognize how that year shaped her into the woman she became. She was able to get off the academic and work treadmill for a year, grow close to her large extended family, live and work in a Latin American city, and fall in love. While she chose to return to the States the following year, those months in Brazil rooted her in her identity and helped her to mature into womanhood. Turns out her "gap year" wasn't a "gap" at all. It was instrumental in helping Brooke orient her priorities, learn about herself and her family, and prepare her to choose her professional life wisely.

Most people won't end up in their dream job straight out of college, or even at the job after that. But the process is just as important as the goal. It sucks to work three jobs so you can pay the rent while interning for free. While your friends are partying Friday night, and you're cleaning up after hours at a restaurant, you might feel sorry for yourself. But in taking ownership of your own life, in making that restaurant a more humane place to work, you start to become an adult who is learning to live like it matters. This chapter has emphasized the beneficial role that imagination plays in the discernment process. But discernment alone cannot solve the mystery of each individual's path. Years after graduation, from the comfortable perch of a satisfying job in advertising, Sofia reflected:

> I believed that if I just thought through the problem enough or considered my options thoroughly, I could arrive at a conclusion. But what I have learned is that until my discernment skills had sharpened with

time and real-life experience, I couldn't necessarily trust my own discernment. Plus, I didn't know what I didn't know, and imagination can't always be a reliable predictor, especially at that early stage of life.

Brooke looks back on her time in college and wishes she had known that she'd have to "kiss a few frogs" (work a few jobs that aren't fulfilling) before finding that dream job in that great location. She had the illusion that just as she had gotten into her top college after hard work, she'd land her dream job just after graduation. When she returned to the States after her gap year abroad, Brooke decided she was ready to try investment banking. Her first job was a nightmare. She only lasted nine months. She switched companies but stayed in Manhattan. The second job was less miserable, her boss was more supportive, but she still felt like a cog in a wheel and life in Manhattan was still insanely expensive. It turns out that she still found her dream job by the time she turned 30—only it was in Austin, Texas, in a startup that gave her more responsibility navigating the finances of the company. Although in Austin she earned much less than in Manhattan, she was able to buy her first place in a year and spent a lot less on day-to-day living. Looking back, Brooke realized that the first jobs she had, while not ideal, certainly taught her a lot about the industry and about where she would eventually serve it. Remember Garrison Keillor took a side job to write for a magazine—a job he didn't particularly like and in which he didn't particularly excel—that led him to that moment at the Grand Ole Opry. It was a moment that inspired him. But then he had to figure out how to channel that inspiration into his own work in radio. He did it, and you can do it too, one step at a time.

Journal Exercise #7

Go back and read through the journal exercises from the last chapter and this chapter. Come up with a plan that helps move you toward the next step in the unfolding of your journey. For some of you, that might mean "find a summer job." For others it might mean "decide on a major." And for others it could mean "decide what job I want to apply for right now."

Remember that you're taking one step in a long journey. Be imaginative. Be curious. Be intentional.

Section 2: Leisure

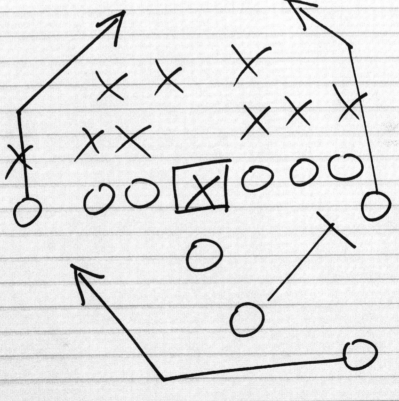

3

Time Wasted

THE ACTIVITIES FAIR

Nobody talks about what a shock it is to arrive at college and have—all of a sudden—hours and hours of free time with no hovering parent. The realization usually comes just a few weeks into the first semester, after homesickness has begun to fade, orientation is over, and some new routines fall into place. A new college student will realize he's got two hours before his next class and nothing to do. *Nothing at all.* Suddenly, there is intense pressure to do *something*, get busy, and be productive. If he doesn't, the sharks—the job market, adult expectations, the future bearing down— might eat him up. Students like Brooke from the work chapters—real and imagined—loom large in the minds of college students. Brooke never wastes time. She's always getting ahead.

College students often respond to this new freedom by getting involved in activities. Here are Brooke's memories about her freshman activities fair that ran two weeks into first semester:

> I remember hearing about the Activities Fair from my Orientation Coun-
> selor. The Activities Fair felt like a gateway to everything that I thought
> college was supposed to be—new friends, constant productivity, and
> a sense of purpose even within moments of free time. I put my email
> address on almost every sign-up sheet, even if I wasn't interested in
> the club or organization. Within a week of the fair, my schedule was

bombarded with meetings, events, and tasks. I was overwhelmed, more overwhelmed than I had ever felt in high school.

By the beginning of October, Brooke's schedule is packed. She's applying to the most prestigious clubs on campus. But midterms collide with all her extracurriculars. And her new sleep schedule—if you can even call it that—isn't helping. Looking back, she has this to say:

> At the beginning of my freshman year, I had several gaps of free time written into my daily schedule. Instead of feeling rejuvenating, these gaps felt ominous. The pressures of high school had been wired into my brain, and I was craving the whirlwind of busyness that I had been accustomed to. I became a product of the myth that free time must be productive, and I was exhausted.

By the time Thanksgiving break rolls around, Brooke is bone tired. She can't keep up with the breakneck pace she has set for herself. When she gets home, she sleeps until mid-afternoon every day to try to recover from the frantic lifestyle she had inadvertently trapped herself into. To her mother's suggestion that she build breaks into her schedule, she thinks, "Anytime someone tells me to slow down or take a break, my knee-jerk reaction is usually, 'Well the other kids in my class are studying for the MCAT, or researching internships or taking on more responsibilities in that club, or. . .'" Here's what she has to say about how she spends her free time:

> Going to a competitive school in the 21st century, it feels difficult to justify any leisure time. I personally have struggled to find meaning in activities beyond academics, fitness, or other explicit forms of 'self-improvement.'

During the hours that she's technically "off"—not studying or doing campus activities—Brooke is managing social media: her Twitter account, binge watching YouTube, or scrolling aimlessly on TikTok. This is enough to keep her busy for a few hours until she falls into bed exhausted. On some weekends she goes out with her dormmates to some party where she doesn't really know anyone. Everyone is drinking a lot—but she won't because she's worried it will affect her school performance. Everyone is taking photos and videos and posting them—but she won't, because she's been warned that employers search social media. As she finds quiet corners and tries to be inconspicuous—she asks herself: *is this all there is?* These activities are supposed to give her a break. Instead, they leave her more dissipated and restless than ever.

How did Brooke and students like her end up in this trap?

Extracurricular activities used to be what you did in your free time. But now "free" time involves opting out of both studying *and* extracurricular activities. So many extracurriculars have become vehicles to build a resume that shows leadership or team building or community involvement. Taking a break means wasting time—on Instagram, TikTok, Netflix, or gaming. But at the end of the scroll or show or game, you may notice that you often feel empty. What's worse, even partying now involves work—what with snapping, curating, and posting photos, followed by liking and commenting on other people's stories. It's exhausting.

How about approaching free time differently? What if instead of time wasted that leaves you feeling anxious and guilty, free time could become an integral part of good living? But the question is: what kind of free time would give you joy? While the key in the work chapters was to set guardrails around work, the key here is to liberate free time. To get out from under the achievement trap, you need to re-center your free time on friendship.

In this chapter, we'll meet students who struggle with centering their lives around real friendship, all while desperately seeking it—through online gaming, social media, and college partying. We'll discuss what these students are really searching for with these apps and activities, and why they often come up empty.

In the next chapter, we'll introduce some practices that will help you reclaim free time, outlining strategies to recenter that time around friendship. We'll see how using free time well is like planting a garden—it involves making a plan, building fences, weeding, planting, and watering.

Let's start by digging into some of the ways college students typically spend their free time.

FREE TIME AS WASTED TIME
Cole's Story

Meet Cole: a college sophomore with a major paper due in a week. It requires some research, but since he's winged papers like this for history classes before, he isn't too concerned. At worst, he'll have to pull an all-nighter to get it done. The prospect of hours spent in front of a computer, reading articles in different journals, taking notes, and preparing an outline feels overwhelming.

Besides, the League of Legends ladder beckons. Cole isn't a great player, but he loves the feeling of gradual improvement. He feels tempted to play League, partially out of a desire to get better, but mostly to avoid having to start his paper.

As he plays, Cole has a few good matches, but the paper weighs on him incessantly. He can't give one hundred percent of his attention to his matches because he still hasn't even started researching. After a few poor matches, Cole stops playing, transferring to YouTube for a vicarious League experience. A few days go by, with Cole attending class, eating, and playing while altogether ignoring the paper rapidly bearing down on him. Cole's friends text him throughout the week asking to hang out. "Can't, I've got this paper due soon," he'd text them. After receiving yet another rejection, Cole's best friend Sean gave up on texting and actually *called* him, for the first time that Cole could remember.

"Cole, where have you been? You've gone MIA," Sean said.

"Sorry, dude. Big paper coming up. We'll hang when I'm done. Umm, better get back to it," Cole replied, staring blankly at League's matchmaking screen. He mumbled something about being in the middle of reading an article for his paper and hung up. After the call, just like every time he turns down his friends, he felt bad about avoiding them for this paper he isn't writing. After classes, he always heads back to his dorm intending to start his paper. But Cole finds himself immediately opening League. He feels trapped.

Eventually, the paper's due date looms just over the horizon. Cole gets stressed because he still hasn't even started the paper. Feeling more anxious than ever, Cole cobbles together a few sources and heads back to his dorm to draft his paper in a rush. The point of the paper is confused, with the cited articles only tangentially relating to the subject at hand. At times Cole finds himself unable to continue writing, unsure of what to say. Day becomes night, and night becomes day. In the morning, Cole finishes working, but the product is not particularly good. He turns in the paper and crashes.

Afterward, Cole realizes that his essay writing process left him unable to devote his full attention either to writing a good essay or practicing League, let alone seeing his friends. He knew that the essay had to be done, but playing games and watching YouTube shorts were much easier. By the time he buckled down to complete the essay, the task really had become overwhelming. Cole could only give a half effort to both activities. Worse, Cole didn't see his friends because he had the essay hanging over him. The way he approached things diminished everything he did. He fell into a vicious cycle of anxiety and avoidance, and it ate an entire week of his life. Before he sees his grade, he thinks that he'd better do things differently next time.

Unfortunately, the professor gives him a decent grade because there were a couple good insights amidst the jumbled arguments. The professor writes that with a little more work, Cole could have done even better. Probably the professor thinks that, by not marking Cole down, she will avoid discouraging him. She is right, but not how she expects. Getting an okay grade allows Cole to justify this habit to himself. He even feels proud that he got the grade he did after having worked on the paper for only a day, and it gives him a more intense high than if he had worked on it a little at a time. Because there are few consequences to his procrastination, his resolve to "do better" is forgotten.

Cole soon finds that this pattern repeats itself. Every time he has something due, he turns down his friends, heads to his room to work, but turns to games instead. The more time he spends gaming, the more stressed he is about his work, the less willing he is to make time for his friends. Sean texts less and less, likely frustrated over Cole's inability to make time for anyone when due dates loom. The game is eating away at his life.

Why does Cole spend so much time gaming? Let's give gaming its due. It offers a sense of teamwork, the thrill of winning, the desire to get better and better at something. It's also a way to relax, have fun, and connect with players. In the end, gaming is fun because you're *playing a game*, instead of being focused on relentless production. Still, it's a huge time suck. And Cole uses it to procrastinate. The sheer amount of time he spends on gaming interferes with his schoolwork. And it keeps him in his room instead of hanging out with friends in real life.

Students like Cole fall into a trap not of their own making. While large companies are making enormous profits on iPhones, monthly phone plans, consoles, and video games, their customers often aren't aware of what exactly they are being sold. Many video games, especially mobile games, are designed to addict users, enticing them into pouring more time and (ideally) money into the game. Tech companies have formed an alliance with unscrupulous behavioral psychologists to keep gamers hooked. To cause addiction, games use "intermittent positive reinforcement." If you've ever opened a loot box or bought a booster pack, you know exactly what this loop feels like. It is anticipation followed by either disappointment or brief elation as your prize is revealed. The randomness of the prizes increases the addictiveness—you never know when you'll hit the jackpot.

These random loop mechanics work like gambling, and they have been ruled as such in other countries, like Belgium and the UK. In a similar fashion, games like League of Legends that require an enormous time investment keep players engaged through intermittent rewards, like level increases or new equipment or cosmetic "skins." These features keep players coming back to the game over and over. But no game advertises these features, because their predatory nature depends on players sleepwalking as they play. You might think you're on a grand adventure, risking your virtual life with the people you're playing with online. But you've actually become a victim of a carefully calculated business strategy fueled by decades of high-end research in behavioral science. Studies show that people who play video games more than a few hours a day are less healthy, less socially connected, and less active. But rather than blaming the game for their dissatisfaction "in real life," addicted gamers turn more and more to the game itself for satisfaction.

Sofia's Story

Now let's hear from Sofia, our English major from the work chapters, back in her early years of college. She is caught in a similar loop as Cole, but with social media. As Sofia approached her freshman year of college, her expectations were through the roof. All summer, she and her high school best friend Kylie discussed their lofty plans for their "brand new lives" at separate colleges. Their hometown afforded few social opportunities aside from the occasional backyard party and the same few love interests they had cycled through. High school academic and social pressures had led them both to struggle with mental health issues. The summer between high school and college, though, their sights were set on new friends, new crushes, new cities, new social prospects.

Since her own college move-in date was in late September, Sofia watched on social media as her high school friends began leaving for college. Her Instagram feed, which was once comfortably full of the same friends and acquaintances she'd seen all her life, was now flooded with her former classmates' new college roommates and friends, people she'd never seen before. And it looked like they were having a lot of fun.

A few weeks after Kylie's departure, her Instagram caption read that she was "living her best life" with friends Sofia had never seen before. Since Kylie basically ghosted Sofia once she left for school (aside from the occasional Snapchat or drunken FaceTime calls where Kylie introduced Sofia to her "new BFFs"), Sofia had to pull information about her life from Instagram. Sofia couldn't help but feel left out and disoriented as her Instagram feed was flooded with more and more strangers.

When it was finally time for Sofia to join the ranks of new college freshmen, she was quickly swept up in the excitement of it all. She had never met so many new people at once. She was exchanging Instagrams and Snapchats with as many people as she could. On the weekends, she attended tailgates, pre-games, and frat parties, posting as many pictures as possible of herself having fun with her "new friends." She would check to make sure Kylie had viewed her Instagram story or liked her post, and she'd compare how many likes her posts received to how many Kylie's posts got. *That will show her for ghosting me!* Sofia thought to herself after uploading yet another blurry selfie with a group of acquaintances and watching the likes accumulate.

Once classes picked up and the ceaseless partying of early fall semester slowed down, Sofia realized that she was worn out. She barely knew the so-called friends in her Insta feed. She also hadn't talked to Kylie in weeks, and she stopped seeing her posts on Instagram. "Has she unfriended me?" Sofia worried at first. But she could still see Kylie's posts—it was only that they had slowed down dramatically, to almost nothing. Sofia didn't think it was one of those "social media cleanses," because obsessive posters tend to post about them before taking a couple weeks off. Kylie's last post of her own was two weeks ago: a photo of her and her sorority "big" decked out in their school's colors at a football game, hugging with big smiles on their faces. There were two reposts without comment since then, neither of which told Sofia anything about Kylie. Kylie *looked* totally happy in the last photo, but the striking halt to her posts alarmed Sofia to the point where she decided to reach out; maybe things weren't what they seemed on Instagram. So, Sofia swallowed her feelings of abandonment and jealousy and called Kylie one evening as she walked home from class.

"Sofia?" Kylie answered the phone, her voice sounding groggy against a quiet background. "Hey Kylie." The other end of the line was silent, except for something that resembled a sniffle, and Sofia wondered if she should just hang up. Things were clearly off between them. She took a deep breath and spoke again, "Look, I just wanted to check in. It looks like you are having so much fun at college without me, but we haven't talked in forever and I really miss you."

"I miss you too," Kylie whispered back, "my friends here are fun but ... being away from home is a lot different than I thought it would be." This time, Sofia definitely heard a sniffle and with Kylie's admission, she felt confident sharing her true feelings, "Yeah ... can I tell you something? I tried to post as much as possible about all the fun I was having. But I really wasn't having that much fun. I just wanted to impress everyone and, um ... prove to you that I was having as a good time as you were. But then your Insta posts stopped, and I guess I got worried, because what if you had gotten depressed again. After last time, I—"

"I am depressed," Kylie said bluntly, and Sofia felt like the wind had been knocked out of her.

"What? Why didn't you tell me?" Sofia said, guilt rising like bile in her stomach as she came to the realization that she hadn't reached out or checked in on Kylie, either.

"I didn't ... look, I'm embarrassed, okay? I am supposed to be having a great time like everyone else but I'm not. Then I'd go on Insta, and you were having so much fun, at least ... it looked like you had so many new friends. I didn't want to bother you. Anyway, I gotta go," Kylie said, and Sofia heard the little beep that meant her former best friend had hung up.

Sofia risked losing a real friend in Kylie. But she risked losing more than that. It's quicker, it's easier, it's more instantly gratifying to post tons of photos on Instagram with new "friends" than to actually invest time into developing real and lasting friendships. Insta friends disappear as quickly as the "delete" button. Social media friends can ghost you as easily as they've friended you. It's much more demanding to seek, find, and keep real friends. As we saw in the first two chapters, productivity sets the terms for *everything*. Young adults don't feel like they have the time, the energy, or even the ability to make and keep real friends. But when they settle for Insta friends over the real thing, they're settling for something fleeting, something fake.

Social media apps like Instagram, Snapchat, or TikTok promise connections with friends, popularity among peers, and real recognition. But in reality, these sites have contributed to the rising tide of depression and anxiety among young people. Feelings of loneliness increased sharply after 2011, just at the time when social media use became widespread. In fact, people who had more frequent social media use and fewer in-person social interactions reported the most loneliness. This is, of course, by design. Like online gaming, many popular social media sites incorporate feedback loops to keep people scrolling or swiping. Because attention can now be commodified, it can also be sold. The longer social media sites hold your attention, the more of your time they can sell to advertisers. Even more insidious, the apps can learn what content to display in order to keep you "engaged." Most people will acknowledge that they spend too much time on their phones, but many aren't aware that addiction is built into their design, just like with video games.

Students are trapped by their phones. "What if my roommates need me?" one student asks. Another says, "If my mom can't reach me, she gets scared that I'm in trouble." Plus, so much of their lives are mediated through their phones. A student like Sofia will say:

> I'd love to be less attached to my phone, but then I'd have no friends, no social life, no way to keep track of the work I have to do, no alarm clock, no step calculator, no access to email. I have to respond through GroupMe, Facebook, or group texts for my class projects and club commitments. My school just created a virtual ID for our phones. So now, without my phone, I couldn't get into the library or dining hall. I basically wouldn't be able to function.

The solution for students like Cole and Sofia isn't to throw away their computers or their phones. (Although we discuss in the next chapter ways to limit the time spent with phones.) They need to opt for something they love more. But first they need to master their relationship to technology, such that the games and apps serve as tools for real friendships. Cole's addiction to League of Legends led him to neglect both his schoolwork and his friendships. Instagram mediated Sofia's relationships to her new college friends and to high school friend, Kylie. What was the result? In substituting Kylie's friendship for superficial Insta friends, Sofia ended up miserable and lonely.

Olivia's Story

Is the solution just to train ourselves away from our screens and hang out with each other instead? That's a first step, for sure, but it's not that easy. It turns out that what you decide to do with your friends matters too. As attractive as the college party scene is at first, it's not a path to real friendships, or real leisure.

Let's meet Olivia, another student struggling with her relationship to leisure. Listen to her recalling her experience with the party scene freshman year:

> I didn't drink a lot in high school, I was so focused on academic excellence and getting into a great college that my social life really took a backseat. When I got to college, the expectation was to go out all the time and drink all the time. Stories of 'blacking out' and not remembering the night before—horror stories, really—are laughed at and celebrated. I had a hard time adjusting to college during my freshman year, so I got into all of these crazy drinking and partying tendencies, thinking this was the best way to fit in and make friends.
>
> When I first got into my sorority, I finally felt like I could relax and start to make friends the old-fashioned way; I was so excited to have some true girlfriends. One night, after an absolutely insane night of drinking, I realized that none of the acquaintances I had made thus far had *actually* cared about me: I was completely blackout drunk, and they allowed me to walk home alone in the cold to try to find my way to my dorm. Totally and completely dangerous and stupid. On my way back, I unknowingly stopped by the door of the boy I liked and knocked on

his door for over thirty minutes just trying to say hello. When I finally got back to my dorm, I vaguely remember putting my pajamas on and getting into bed to go to sleep. A few minutes later, I got another call from a girl in my sorority saying that she was going out again and she wanted me to come. I was desperate for friends and totally wracked by FOMO—so I decided to go. She told me I had ten minutes to get changed and get in the Uber. So, I hopped out of bed and grabbed a pair of jeans and started to put them on.

That's when I accidentally jumped and landed wrong on my foot. Pain shot through my foot; I couldn't even stand up on it correctly. But the Uber was coming, and Abigail was waiting. So I shimmied into my jeans, grabbed my Converse, and limped, barefoot, down the stairs to the Uber. I got into the Uber screaming and crying while Abigail tried to lace up my shoes over my massive foot that was quickly turning black and blue.

When we got to the party, I was crying so hard that right when I got in the doors, everyone thought I was absolutely insane. A boy that lived in my dorm saw me and insisted that he take me home. He picked me up, carried me bridal style to the Uber that he called for me, and tossed me into the Uber to go back to my dorm.

Upon arriving at my dorm, I was so drunk and in so much pain that I managed to piss off every one of my friends by being a total jackass on the way up to my room. The next morning, I woke up and went to Urgent Care.

After finding out that my foot was broken, I hobbled back to my room on crutches and in a boot. I had managed to alienate the very few friends I had, the boy I liked would not talk to me anymore, and I walked into a sorority meeting the next day on crutches. I had never felt so alone.

The next week or so, everyone seemed to be mad at me. I was just trying to get through the days, on crutches, feeling oh-so alone. I'm not saying that drinking ruined my life. Sure, I participated in underage drinking and got a little too out of hand. But the real problem was thinking that *this* was the only way to make connections. Doing it not because I wanted to, but because I felt that I had to. And then, when the shit hit the fan and the dust cleared, I realized that I hadn't made any meaningful connections by doing this. Spending my leisure just trying to fit in had actually put me more on the outskirts.

Students tell us that not only is the party scene exhausting, but the social media component of partying makes it worse because you have to snap and curate and post constantly. There's more. Much like Instagram or gaming, partying gives young adults the false sense that they are carefree, that they can have "honest" conversations because they're wasted. Its liquid courage provides cover for late night confessions that can just as easily be disavowed the next morning. And drinking as self-medication to cover loneliness and insecurity expires in hours. Here's one student talking about this experience:

> Binge drinking seems like a good idea because it helps boost my confidence, reduce my insecurities, and forget about other life obligations to allow me to loosen up and meet new people. However, in reality, binge drinking is not good for my physical or mental health, and I usually wake up with a headache and hangxiety the next morning. Yet, after drinking some Pedialyte and taking a long shower, I am ready to do it again and face the same consequences. I won't lie that I like being drunk: it makes me feel brave and invincible. My drunk self can talk to people I am intimidated by and have the tough conversations that my sober self can't, and I think that's why I like the feeling. I am jealous of my drunk self in a way because she is able to take the plunge without double (or triple) checking how far the fall is. The cycle of overthinking how people might perceive me is definitely something I can improve by working on myself (while sober) but as long as I have alcohol as a crutch, I know I won't put in the work. Binge drinking is not actually a good habit for me, it just makes me feel good in the moment, so I chase the feeling.

While gaming, earbuds, social media, and drinking provide temporary buffers to young adults seeking real friendships, at the end of the day or in the clear light of morning, they're still lonely. They still want real friendship. They yearn to belong. Moving away from virtual connection and toward real friendships is hard.

In the next chapter, we'll give you some tips to help you cultivate the necessary habits to make this hope for friendship a reality. But first, let's reimagine how we think about leisure in order to bring to the center what belongs there: friendship with yourself and others.

FREE TIME AS LEISURE TIME

Good living is like bodily health. Think of how many times you've been told that diet affects your ability to exercise, and that your exercise routine makes you eat better. Not getting enough sleep causes stress and anxiety levels to spike. And drinking water makes basically everything better. In short, your body, mind, and spirit are deeply interconnected, such that when you fall off the exercise routine, you stop sleeping as well, your anxiety gets out of control, and you eat poorly out of stress and exhaustion.

Leisure practices are embedded in this network of healthy living, and they can either bring you into balance or throw you off-kilter. Here's 30-year-old Brooke, once she's moved to Austin and settled into her dream job:

> On a good day, leisure time is reading books, working out, going on walks or hikes, calling my friends. On a bad day, leisure time is zoning out on TikTok for an hour or watching Netflix but not even paying attention. Leisure time for me reminds me of Newton's First Law—an object in motion will stay in motion. When I'm doing things that fill me up, like reading or exercising, it's easier to keep doing those things. Likewise, when I'm feeling apathetic and end up scrolling on TikTok or Instagram, it's easy to keep doing that, and harder to motivate myself to do something else.

Over time, leisure practices shape you into the person you are, at least as much as what you do for work. *At least* as much. And yet, when we bring up the word "leisure" in college seminars, most students look at us with blank stares until one of them says, "What's that?"

We might take a cue from observant Jews, who preserve true leisure practices in their weekly routine. Twentieth-century Rabbi Abraham

Heschel argues that Judaism's great gift to the world was the Sabbath: "the Sabbaths are our great cathedrals," he writes. Walter Brueggemann adds that the Sabbath is about "the refusal to let one's life be defined by production and consumption and the endless pursuit of private well-being."

Remember the story from Genesis in chapter 1? Even before Genesis became a story about work, it was a story about being alive. God creates the world in six days and rests on the seventh. This day of rest is the culmination of the work that went before it. It's not a pause between work and work. It didn't come on a Wednesday. Instead, it's a day for the sake of life, offering an opportunity, as Heschel writes, "to mend our tattered lives." The weekdays serve the Sabbath, which "is not an interlude but the climax of living." This day makes us grateful to be alive. It makes us stop and focus on our relationships. The Sabbath is at the heart of leisure. And yet this is exactly the *opposite* way that we think about leisure when we think of it as a rest that serves work.

It is not until the next chapter of Genesis that Adam and Eve are put to work. Their work grows out of that same gift of being alive. They become stewards of the garden of creation. In fact, work allows you to make room in your life for what isn't work—leisure activities that bring you into realignment with the world. Observant Jews show what leisure really means by not using electricity or iPhones or email on the Sabbath.

We've seen that work is an important element in a good life—through meaningful productive work, a person fulfills her potential by developing her unique capacities. Rest provides a much-needed break from work, like plugging in a rechargeable battery that's been depleted. But you only recharge your battery to put it to work again. Leisure is not about getting recharged for work; it's about free time worth having.

Journal Exercise #9

Think about how you spend your free time—time that you aren't working or doing extracurriculars that have begun to feel like "work." Write down a list of activities you love to do during your free time. Circle the top three that you do the most and write about why you do them and how you feel after doing them.

Leisure time is filled with activities and relationships we pursue for their own sake, for the sheer joy of it.

Let's take a step back and look at a fictional story that helps us see what it's like to have what really matters at the center. Great stories allow us to see the world differently—as it truly is. With love at the center, *everything* we do, whether for work or leisure, serves a life well-lived.

FREE TIME AS FEAST

"Babette's Feast" is a short story by the Danish author Isak Dinesen. (It is also a celebrated Danish film, winner of the 1988 Oscar for best foreign film.) Her story takes place in a small town in Norway sometime in the middle of the 1800s. Martine and Philippa are two elderly sisters who never married. Their deceased father had been the leader of a Puritan religious group who insisted that their members renounce all the pleasures of this world.

At first glance, Martine and Philippa could not be more different than Brooke, Cole, and Sofia. Overprogrammed, overworked, and sometimes-overwhelmed college students struggling with Fortnite or Instagram don't seem to have much with two elderly women living in an isolated Norwegian village in the 1870s. But on second glance, there are deep similarities. For both the characters of the story and for young adults today, the world is scarce and scary. Both groups respond by fearing risk and seeking control. The result is lost opportunity and loneliness. The world often does seem scarce and scary. But the response to that scarcity makes a world of difference. The main character in the story, Babette, responds differently. In the face of tragedy, she takes a risk; she travels alone to a foreign country, shows up to a stranger's doorstep, and asks for shelter and work.

"Babette's Feast" opens with a description of a Puritan community in a cold and remote northern European port. The congregants are getting older and grayer, and they are not attracting new members. They begin to bicker with each other, producing "sad little schisms." So the community shrinks every year.

Martine and Philippa come of age in this community. As young women both were extraordinarily attractive. Their beauty is even called "supernatural." Lots of young men were interested in them. But their father—who had his daughters late in life—refused to give them away. He insisted to himself that they had been brought up for heavenly not earthly love.

In time, Martine falls in love with young army officer Lorens who comes to town to visit relatives. Lorens feels the same. He wants to tell Martine that he loves her. But he feels unworthy of her and can't bring himself to do it. So, instead, he says goodbye forever. "Fate is hard and there are impossible things in this life," he tells her. He leaves the town to focus on his career in the army, trading love for professional success. He moves quickly up in the ranks and marries one of the queen's ladies in waiting. But Lorens never forgets Martine.

Something similar happens to Philippa. One day, a famous and handsome opera singer, Papin, comes to town from Paris and hears Philippa sing in church. Smitten by both her beauty and her voice, he offers her music lessons. He's convinced she can develop her talents to the point where she can become a famous singer. After singing a duet together during a lesson, Papin kisses her. Philippa freaks out and tells her father she doesn't want any more lessons. She is "surprised and frightened by something in her own nature." "Her nature" includes her sexuality and her singing talent. She decides to give up both. Her suitor leaves, and she never sees him again.

This early part of the story is marked by unfulfilled longing, forsaken love, and lost potential. The young people in this story have thrown away their best possibilities because they're convinced that life isn't generous enough to give them what they really long for. All of this lost potential comes from the same source—a fearful attitude towards the world. Both Martine and Philippa let the fear of risk drive their decisions. In the face of uncertainty and fear, they give up on the possibility of joy.

One day fifteen years later, Babette, a refugee from a revolution in France, lands at their door. Babette is "haggard and wild eyed like a hunted animal." She'd been arrested and lost all her possessions, fleeing France after her husband and son were shot. For Babette, the world is definitely scarce and scary. But she faces her fears and moves to a foreign country to make a new life there.

She carries a letter from the opera singer Papin asking Martine and Philippa to take her in. The letter assures them that Babette can cook. The sisters can't afford her. But Babette pleads with them—if they send her away she will die. So they relent and take her into their home. This is the first time in the story that Martine and Philippa take a real risk, but this risk comes barging into their lives pleading with them to take her in.

Twelve years later, Babette wins a considerable sum in a lottery. The sisters have come to love her and are worried that this new wealth will make Babette leave. It's easy to understand why. The huge earnings could allow her to retire and move back to France. Instead, Babette asks the sisters to allow her to cook a meal. "A real French dinner," she says. They don't like the sound of this. But Babette assures them she will pay for the dinner with her winnings:

> Martine and Philippa looked at each other. They did not like the idea; they felt that they did not know what it might imply. But the very strangeness of the request disarmed them.

So they reluctantly agree. This is the second time in the story that the sisters take a risk.

As there's no Amazon Prime yet, Babette has to travel for ten days to order all the ingredients. The sisters are increasingly upset as they see all sorts of weird food show up, including a live turtle. They tell their friends that when they come to dinner, they should ignore all the bizarre food to spare Babette's feelings. The sisters, while having agreed to the risk of the meal, prepare themselves and their guests for the worst. Their fears are still driving the way they approach this feast.

By chance, Lorens, who had left Martine to climb the military ladder, is also in town and gets himself invited to dinner. He's now a distinguished general in the army. Being familiar with fine dining, Lorens is effusive in praising Babette's dishes. The other guests had promised the sisters they wouldn't say a word about the food. But the excellent food and wine begin to loosen their tongues. They remember the old preacher fondly and recall all the acts of kindness the sisters had done for the congregation over the years. Two of the old men who had held a grudge for years apologize to each other and become reconciled. An old widow and widower who had fallen in love when they were young but married other people instead now wind up kissing each other. General Lorens is so moved by the dinner and the friendly atmosphere that he says:

> We tremble before making our choice in life, and after having made it
> again tremble in fear of having chosen wrong. But the moment comes
> when our eyes are opened, and we see and realize that grace is infinite.
> Grace, my friends, demands nothing from us but that we shall await it
> with confidence and acknowledge it in gratitude.

Lorens names the fear that has been driving all the members of the congregation up to this point. Each member has chosen a smaller life because they were afraid to take a risk and ask more from life. But Lorens points out that, as the meal has shown them, life is an abundant gift to be embraced not feared. And embracing abundance leads to more abundance.

At the end of the meal, the old guests go out into the snow on a starry night. It's like they'd been given a taste of heaven. They laugh and play on their way home like they're little children again.

Martine and Philippa walk into the kitchen to thank an exhausted and happy Babette. They learn that she spent all of her winnings on the meal, and they exclaim that she shouldn't have spent all she had for their sake. Babette responds that she had cooked so that she could once again do what she was born to do. They learn that until her arrest she'd been a famous chef in Paris. They lament how poor she is now. "I am a great artist," she says. "A great artist is never poor."

Babette's approach to the world is very different from Lorens, or the sisters, or the older members of the congregation. Each of these renounced the world, believing it to be hostile to their deepest hopes and desires. Each let fear drive their life's decisions. Each denied themselves the opportunity to reach out for what they really desired. Some of the characters make this mistake because of their religious convictions. Philippa does it because she is afraid of her sexual desire and what it would demand of her. Ambition drives Lorens's decision, as he confines "success" to climbing the ladder of prestige and wealth. All of these characters share the same attitude towards the world. This attitude about a dark and stingy world is at the heart of our contemporary cultural problem with work and leisure.

Babette's love of cooking comes from a very different place. She uses the gift of the lottery and the gift of her talent to prepare a meal so overwhelmingly good that it reconnects the guests to the pleasures of food and to each other. She takes her lottery winnings and turns them into a gift for others because she loves her work. It was meaningful. Spending her leisure time on this meal fills her tank. She spends the gift of the lottery winnings on others, in gratitude for the risk they took so many years ago when inviting her in. Was what Babette did that night a lot of work? Of course. Was it leisure? Absolutely. Leisure, as we said before, does not just mean rest. Her leisure activity was powered by the same energy for living that had gone into her years of service. And so should yours.

FREE TIME AS FRIENDSHIP

In "Babette's Feast," the desire to minimize risk has devastating consequences for the relationships the author portrays. The sisters come to fear love and sex, choosing control instead. As we'll see in the romance chapters, erotic love is risky. Lorens is afraid that falling in love will ruin his ambitions, so he shuts that door. He settles instead for the 19th century version of the achievement trap: a busy, loveless climb up the greasy pole of military "success." Because they're afraid of the world with all its real risks and sacrifices, Martine, Philippa, and Lorens lead a life that closes in on itself. Their choices about the world and their relationships end up affecting the way they relate to themselves as well. And the way they treated themselves was reflected in the friendships they had—or didn't have.

Friendship is challenging and risky—it involves the risk of opening yourself up to another person. It's easier to post a fabulous picture on Instagram that projects fun, confidence, and popularity than it is to seek out real people with whom to create connections and memories. How much of our attraction to Instagram or online gaming is actually a desire to control our relationships? Online gaming can challenge your mental and physical dexterity, but it's also a way of feeling the thrill of risk all from the safety of your own room, often hiding behind an avatar or a fake name. If you settle for social media and gaming, you are actually settling for virtual relationships that provide the illusion of intimacy and control instead of real friendships that involve work, risk, and great reward. Nights of heavy drinking, oddly enough, can also be a form of self-protection: "I was so wasted" is regularly used to excuse us from the responsibilities of our actions. The invincible-seeming "drunk me" becomes a mask hiding the vulnerable "sober me." Again, the right response to all this isn't to just stop wasting time and be more productive, as the Brookes of the world try to do. It's to reset what happens when we're not being "productive"—it's to reclaim free time in a way that really makes us free.

At the end of the story we could ask whether the feast that Babette put together was for her own happiness? Or was it solely a way to thank her hosts who had saved her during a desperate time? But it's the result of our social imaginary (see chapter 2) that we'd even ask these questions. Our culture offers a false dichotomy between working on ourselves and being directed toward others. The "self-care" industry wants us to think that living for others means not caring for ourselves, which must be remedied with bath bombs, face masks, and other "me time" pleasures. Babette does not use her lottery winning to "treat herself." Her supreme act of loyalty and sacrifice turns out to be what makes her most happy. We will see in the next chapter that at the heart of true leisure practices lies a grateful attitude toward the world that finds expression in community. Leisure isn't only oriented inwardly toward the self. It is directed outward, toward family, friends, and the world around us. In directing our lives outward, not to impress people but to really know them, to help them and to accept help from them, we find inner joy.

The response is to re-center. It's to ask more from free time; not less. And that re-centering starts and ends with love. This is the great paradox of love—we discover the meaning of our lives when we realize that there are things more important than we are. When we devote ourselves to these people and these things, we find ourselves again.

Think back to those journaling exercises earlier in the chapter. When did you most feel "yourself"? When you were posting a photo on Instagram? Or when you lost yourself in a good novel? When you were online gaming? Or when you played pickup basketball? Becoming an adult means learning to love activities and people beyond yourself. As we'll learn more in the chapter 5, love isn't just a warm feeling. It's the consistent desire to care for the good of another. When we learn to care about our real friends or devote ourselves to developing our love for art or music or sports, we are carried out of ourselves in a way that makes us more deeply who we really are. It helps us discover our true identity.

Love is risky. But it's at the heart of a good life.

Every story in this chapter revolves around friendship and community. Gaming and social media aim at friendship, but in limited ways, so they turn attention back to the self. Cole wants to play with friends instead of writing his paper, but gaming only half-satisfies that longing. Freshman Sofia is so obsessed with looking like she has friends that she makes no friends. But it is not enough to stop gaming and turn off your phone or Apple watch. Olivia's drunken desperation for friendship leads her to a broken foot and loneliness. Babette's story is different. She loses herself in her cooking, the guests lose themselves in the meal, and this heals their community. Babette gives over her creativity, her skill, and her money to her hosts and their friends. Cooking fulfills her. But it is in sharing the fruits of her passion that she's truly satisfied.

To become like Babette, you need to free yourself from the achievement trap and start living like it matters. We saw how this can reorient your approach to work in the last chapters. But it should also reframe your approach to leisure. Crafting an intentional approach to leisure includes examining your relationship to alcohol, the quality of your friendships, and the activities that you choose to do in your free time.

The next chapter will provide some practical tools to rehabilitate your leisure time. In the romance chapters you'll learn that love pulls you out of yourself. This is true with leisure, too—because it always involves things or people you love. Leisure draws us into the world of other people, of nature, of art, of music. It harmonizes you with the world around you. *That's why friendship lies at the heart of leisure time.* With friends, you forget about time. With friends, you forget about yourself. With friends, you get lost in whatever activity you're doing together.

4

Time Saved

FREE TIME AS FLOW

This chapter will help you examine how you spend your free time. We'll invite you to recall activities that you did when you were younger but that might have gotten sidelined by the achievement trap. You'll begin to recover these and discover other ways to spend your time that recenter your life on what is truly important to you.

Rethinking your relationship to free time will free you up for deeper, more realistic relationships with the world and the people you love. It takes time and practice to work our way into these new relationships. Living like it matters is a goal, but it's also a process, one that will go in fits and starts. It involves taking stock and being truthful about where you are and what progress you've made. If we aren't being truthful with ourselves, we won't make real progress.

Think of being faced with a free two hours. Option one: sit on your couch and scroll through social media or YouTube. Option two: going for a hike with friends. Which is a more fulfilling way to "spend" those two hours? One is sedentary, the other active. One leaves you at best feeling amused, but more likely, feeling restless and depleted. The other may also leave you tired, but the good kind of tired that comes from exercise and fresh air. One is solitary, the other social.

Or should those two "free hours" be filled with extra work? As we saw in chapter 2, overwork becomes a problem when we don't have our priorities straight. If we don't set up guardrails around work, it overtakes our lives. Work should serve a wider life. It doesn't belong at the center. But if our center is empty, work or study rush in to fill the vacuum.

We ask the same question here that we asked in the work chapters: *what kind of life does our free time serve?* Love is at the center of human living. For everyone. It blossoms in distinctive ways in each person. This isn't just "my truth." It's "our truth." Living love means different things depending on where you are in life and what you have to do—and it will change as you get older. But all along, your loves should be at the center of who you are—the people, work, and activities you love.

Imagine a crisp, sunny fall afternoon. You and your friends decide to head down to the local park for a game of touch football. No parents are involved. No refs. No uniforms and no field. Just you and your friends in an open space surrounded by brilliant fall colors. The game is fun. Sometimes people drop passes, or there's an argument about whether someone was out of bounds. But it's all exhilarating. Before you know it, the sun is down, and you head home for dinner. But as you walk away from the field laughing and jostling each other, tossing the football around, you feel connected, happy, and alive. When you get home, you're amazed that you'd been playing for three hours. It felt like twenty minutes.

Journal Exercise #10

Think back to the last time you weren't working and yet were really joyful.
- What were you doing?
- Who were you with?
- Why were you happy?

Write down as many details of that moment as you can. How long did that happiness last?

Can you think back to an experience like this? Maybe it was a time when you went to a great movie followed by a terrific conversation over drinks with your best friends. Or when went to the local festival in town to ride the rides, check out the sights, and eat cotton candy. It doesn't have to be a social event, especially if you're an introvert. Maybe it was a time when you wrote in your journal all afternoon, or lost yourself in a really good book, or went for a run through the park. Maybe you like to paint. Or knit. What matters is that the time away from work didn't feel measured, planned, controlled. Nor did it feel addicted, compulsive, trapped. It felt free.

Notice in the journal exercise what the conditions were that made you feel happy. People who have done this exercise say that it was their friends or the event or the moment that made them happy. Very rarely does a student point to a *thing* and say, "That made me happy." If it's bubble tea, it's not the actual tea, but rather that Sofia went with her roommate Brooke to this tea place whenever they were too stressed out to study. The place became special because their friendship made it so.

What distinguishes activities you do to waste time from leisure activities? We've already said that the former leaves you dissipated, lonely, anxious, and depressed, while the latter leaves you feeling energized, fulfilled, and connected. But how can we break out of patterns of wasting time, especially with activities that are *designed* to be addictive? How can we cultivate healthier patterns?

The first place to look is what you liked to do as a kid. Leisure is not sitting around doing nothing. It is doing something you enjoy without the burden of trying to do it well. Like when you were young. The achievement trap succeeds in stamping out your childhood playfulness by the time you're in college or certainly as you begin full-time work. It's time to recover a sense of play.

To help us decrease our passive consumption and increase active free time, let's highlight general features of the kind of activities we're encouraging you to do. Psychologist Mihály Csíkszentmihályi—let's call him "Dr. C."—was born in the 1930s in what is now Croatia. During World War II he spent time in an Italian prison camp where he learned to play chess. He found that this game helped him to ignore what was happening around him, which in turn ensured that he fared better than others in the camp. That formative childhood experience stayed with him years later when he wrote his most important work, *Flow: The Psychology of Optimal Experience.* He argues there that people are happy when they achieve a state of "flow," a kind of intrinsic motivation that keeps one fully focused on the situation or task. Flow happens when a person is completely immersed in an activity for the sheer delight of it. We say "time flies when you're having fun"—this usually happens during flow. It is called "flow" rather than just "fun" because of how one action and movement seems to flow into the next, as if you're an expert musician playing a piece without a pause. Your whole existence is at play in the activity and *all* your gifts are being used. If there is effort involved, it's a smooth, satisfying effort, not a grinding toil.

In this chapter, we encourage you to examine your leisure activities and find those in which you experience flow. Then make sure to make time for these in your daily or weekly schedule. Let's look at an experience of flow in Sofia's junior year of college.

Sofia is facing her most difficult year of school yet. On top of a rigorous course load, she works at a competitive internship two days a week, babysits for some extra cash, and is an editor for the college newspaper.

She tries to wind down on weekends by going out with her friends like she did as a freshman, but keeping up with her party-loving friends and the drama that comes along with it can feel like another job in itself.

One day, Sofia notices an ad for a recreational softball league in the college paper. Joining this league becomes her escape from her many stresses. Sofia always loved softball and played competitively growing up, but by the time high school was over she was so burnt out with the constant need to impress her coaches and compete with teammates for scholarships that she quit the game. But joining this rec league allows Sofia to play casually once a week with other students who love the game. Once Sofia puts on her cleats and visor and hits the field each Saturday, time breezes past as she gets in the zone—pitching, fielding, hitting, running the bases—and she hasn't felt so free in a long time—maybe ever. The feeling when she gets a hit or makes a catch in the field is simply unmatched, especially because she's met with cheers and high-fives from her teammates. She hopes to hit a home run before the season is over.

Sofia experiences "flow" during these softball games. Softball includes clear, achievable goals. In any given rec game, Sofia knows what the goal is. Tangible feedback is also important for flow. The moment the ball makes contact with her bat, she knows whether she's nailed it. This particular league enables a balance between opportunity and capacity; that is, it provides enough room for growth without being too difficult. If her team is completely outclassed by the other team, she's just going to experience frustration during the game. Flow activities demand deep concentration such that there is no temptation to check her phone every couple of minutes. This leads to an altered sense of time where she loses herself in the activity, and she basically forgets about herself. She sinks completely into what she's doing. Sofia takes off her Smart watch during these games, knowing she won't need it. Finally, while she does not have complete control over what will happen, she does know what is expected of her. Whenever Sofia walks out onto the field, she knows what her role is in relation to her teammates, and she knows exactly where she needs to place her concentration.

When you're experiencing flow, you'll notice that most of these conditions hold true.

Dr. C maintains that while people *say* they want leisure, the overwhelming number experience flow way more often at work than during leisure. The experience of flow in work is another indicator that a job might be right for you because flow allows you to experience the meaningfulness of work without constantly thinking about what you're

Journal Exercise #11
Dr. C. lists 8 characteristics necessary for a "flow" activity:
- Clear goals
- Immediate feedback
- Balanced opportunity and capacity
- Deep concentration
- Being in the present
- Control
- Altered sense of time
- Egolessness

Think of an experience in which you've been in a state of "flow." What was the memory that popped into your mind first? Write about this memory. This can be during any activity you have done. No need to restrict yourself to things we'd consider "leisure." What were the conditions you met during this flow experience?

getting out of it. As far as leisure goes, there is a difference for most of us between what we think we want and how we actually structure our lives. After obsessing about the college admissions process, once on campus many students obsess over majors and internships and job prospects with literally no attention to leisure other than those activities related to health and wellness.

So, the first step in rehabilitating free time is to notice where you experience flow in your leisure time, or, more commonly, when you used to experience flow. These will form the beginning building blocks to success in this aspect of your adult life.

BUILDING YOUR GARDEN

We've described how the demand for achievement tries to fill up every waking minute, until the need for "down time" comes crashing in. When the center of our lives is achievement, this down time seems to be wasted. And unfortunately, you'll see that much free time among your fellow students *is* wasted. To help us think about how we can make better use of free time, let's switch metaphors from time to space. Recentering your life around free time is like planting a garden in your yard.

Developing fruitful leisure habits is a lot like gardening a patch of land. Gardening itself is for many people a flow activity. The gardener has clear goals, perhaps to grow cucumbers and tomatoes. He receives tangible feedback when the seeds begin to grow. He can become better at nurturing his plants and flowers, more attentive to the things that are working and the plants that are wilting or developing disease. When he gardens, he is completely present to the activity, losing a sense of time. The beginner gardener has a reasonable amount of control over the activity, assuming it matches his level of expertise.

So, imagine your free time as a garden. In this image, you are the gardener—you are in charge of using your free time to cultivate a place where you can be yourself, taking time for activities that give you rest, feed your soul, and connect you to the world around you. You'll plant your favorite flowers. Or plant fresh tomatoes and cucumbers. As you begin to cultivate leisure practices that produce flow, you'll be acting much like a gardener, trying to turn a weedy patch of land into one that produces fruits, vegetables, and flowers.

Gardening isn't always fun. There's weeding, tilling, and fertilizing. You have to deal with pests and animals that might come along to try to eat what you've planted. Sometimes you have to put up fences to keep destructive things out. And the fruits of your labor will be unexpected. Some plants will take root and multiply. Others will wilt and die. The success of the garden isn't entirely up to you. The natural conditions in the soil will encourage some plants to grow and inhibit others from growing. The surprises are part of the point. But in the end, it will be worth the work, patience, and perseverance.

The next pages in our playbook show you how to cultivate leisure like you would a garden.

Build a Fence

All gardens start with a plan. You have to choose the best spot in your yard and most likely build a fence to keep the rabbits and deer out. It's also crucial to build a fence around your free time. Set aside little "sabbaths" that you'll protect from encroachment by work. Think about the times of day you are more alert, awake, or active. Take stock of your typical day. What time could you set aside as free time, time that won't be gobbled up by other obligations? What are your weekends like?

The most important fence to build here is one that keeps your phone out. Your phone is a garden super-predator, ready to devour all of your free time if you let. Even if you manage not to look at it, your brain can still be distracted, knowing that it's ready at hand. Turn off notifications to social media or email—to as many apps as possible, really. At night, plug it in somewhere either out of your bedroom or away from your night table. Buy a cheap alarm clock to wake you up. Stop using your phone for exercise. You don't need to count your steps to become active. If you read for leisure, put your phone—and maybe even your Smart watch—in another room or in a drawer. Here's someone who started to protect herself against the social media predator:

> It's been 6 weeks since I deleted Snapchat. I kind of wanted to do it all summer because it was feeling like a full time job to "keep up" with what everyone was doing, and then the first few days I was having major FOMO of what everyone else was doing and I realized I was making myself miserable for no reason. I will never go back to Snapchat. Life has been so much easier without it. I can't believe I used to wake up and the first thing I did was look through all the fun everyone had had the night before—I was literally setting myself up for failure. The other big realization is that I haven't missed out on anything. Also, it's actually refreshing to see someone and ask them how their day was and not already know what happened to them. You get so much more out of connecting with them in-person. These realizations all seem obvious, but what I've learned about myself is that I can't half-ass the social

media cleanse thing. I don't have the willpower to have the app on my phone and not use it. I have to go for the whole delete.

Everyone needs to protect themselves from being overtaken by their phones. Everyone. Put your phones away in another room while you're reading a favorite book. Leave it in your dorm room or in your car. Learn how to use "Do Not Disturb" settings to let your parents or close friends reach you if necessary, but no one else. If there's one app you need, download it and temporarily disable the Internet so that you can't use the distracting ones. When you can, turn it all the way off while you're spending leisure time.

Another "predator" might be the achievement trap itself. Here is someone who articulates what this looks like:

> I often impose a strict schedule and to-do list upon myself. The intent is to be more productive and do more in less time so that in the remaining hours of the day I can enjoy my life. But the to-do list always slips into the hours I had previously labeled as "free time" and intended for leisure. Before I know it, it's 3 a.m., and I just finished my schoolwork or the slide deck my manager requested. Usually, I end up in this situation because I simply couldn't tear myself away from the project I'm working on. Good is never "good enough."

Journal Exercise #12
Come up with a "fence plan" with respect to technology. Think about what is the worst "predator" attacking your garden. Design a plan to protect your garden. Check in on your plan in 7 days and reassess.

Or maybe your "predator" is your tendency to let your part-time job gobble up all available unclaimed hours. If your manager asks you what free times you have to work in a given week, know that just because you're free doesn't mean you're available to work an extra shift at your job.

Weed It

Screens are part of the problem. They're also a symptom, of not knowing what else to do or of wanting to avoid negative emotions. Start to weed them out of your life. Look at weekly screen time reports. Keep a log. Improve. Try going to a party or place and NOT taking and posting a photo on Instagram. Just be present and enjoy where you are. If you want to convince your friends to do this with you, show up with a disposable camera. Sure, phones can make us more productive—on the front end. But on the back end, they suck it right out. That "minute" you went on Instagram just turned into twenty without you even noticing. Take an app cleanse. Notice how you feel. If you find binge scrolling through TikTok is your time suck, delete it for a week. If it's gaming that sucks you in, put your console in another person's room for 7 days and see how you feel at the end of the week. If you and your friends sit down to watch a movie on Netflix, but you're all also on your phones scrolling, put those phones away.

The most important thing is not any particular rule—or how often you mess it up—but to be attentive to how the presence of the phone affects you. Is it helping or hurting? If it's still hurting, keep taking evasive actions until you can honestly say that you've protected your free time and attention.

Seed It

You've already got seeds to plant. Remember Sofia's desire for real friendship? She and Kylie were best friends in high school. She needs to find a best friend in college. Cole might decide to eliminate single-player gaming and only allow himself to game with friends he's met in person. This on its own will limit the time that gets gobbled up with gaming, because they won't always be available. He might join a basketball league with his friends to make sure he gets outside and interacts in real time with them. Cole might actually like participating in one of the clubs he's chosen, but he should reduce his overall commitments and focus on the ones in which he really experiences flow. Students recall that they used to crochet or play football or write music or paint, but that they haven't picked up a sheet of music or paint brush in years, or their guitar sits in the corner of their room gathering dust. Young adults actually have seeds that are ready to be replanted. They're often just forgotten. Here's one student recalling how she loved to read as a kid:

> I was a big bookworm as a kid. I know lots of people will say this but it's true in my case. I would bring a book everywhere I went with my family. At the mall, head down. At the zoo, head down. At my sister's soccer game, head down. When I was nine or ten, my mom had to move the bookshelves out of my room so I wouldn't stay up until sunrise and

then consequently miss the bus and act cranky in the classroom. After that, I would just lie there, staring up at my ceiling with a glow-in-the-dark constellation of stars and think. I would mess around with the plotlines I was already familiar with or crossover the characters, occasionally adding in people from my own life. I would edit the ending to better fit my tastes, add an epilogue, or maybe even create new stories all together.

Unfortunately, as screens invade kids' lives at ever-earlier points, these experiences of childhood flow are becoming scarcer, too. You may have to dig deep into your past—a family vacation, a sleepaway camp—to find a time when you experienced genuine flow.

Journal Exercise #13

Let's take a trip down memory lane. Close your eyes. Sit up straight. Take a couple of deep breaths to clear your mind.
• What did you love doing as a preschooler?
• What about when you were in elementary school?
• What did you do outside school?
• What did you do with your friends?
• What practices did you have as a kid that you might have lost in high school or college?

Write these down. Circle the ones you want to recover. Write a commitment plan to recover them.

Plant It

As with gardening, building up a life of genuine leisure takes time. Start small. Plant the seeds. Check planting dates (when is it time to sign up for new activities or quit others). Learn your frost dates (are there events that tend to draw you back to social media or times of year when you feel more in need of a "hit"?) Don't try to read *War and Peace* during the semester. Learn when you're most apt to start a new exercise regime. Figure out when friends have more time for daytime socializing.

College is a great time to experiment in living well. Take a course for the fun of it. Take an architectural history course or an urban planning course so that you can learn how to walk through a new city and appreciate the buildings, notice how the streets are laid out in relation to each other and whether they build real community. Take art history or music appreciation or astronomy. When thinking about your "extra-curriculars," be brutally honest with yourself about why you are there and how it impacts you. Volunteering at a homeless shelter so you can put it on your resume is actually all about you. Remember how love works—you have to devote yourself to the good of something else for it to actually come back to you. Maybe continue volunteering, but don't list it on your resume. See how that changes you.

The key is to focus on something you want to do for its own sake. Not to be more productive. Not to impress anyone. Just because it helps others and gives you joy. This can actually be a training ground to change your attitude towards work, too, in the way that we described in the first two chapters.

Another successful strategy to cultivate leisure is to start scheduling a game night with your friends. Here's Sofia talking about a game night she and her friends began:

> When I was a junior, I started to become more involved in the service frat on campus, and after going to the club bonding events, I became really close with the other members. During one night of heavy drinking, we all admitted to each other that we had loved playing the game "Settlers of Catan" with our friends and families growing up. We started jostling with each other about who could build the largest settlements. By the end of the night, we decided we'd start playing regularly. So throughout the fall semester, we would get together once a week to play Catan. It was the first time in college I had ever done any kind of "fun/hang out activity" that was planned around something other than drinking. We eventually got a group of around seven of us who consistently played every Tuesday night. It became such a fun tradition: we would play the game a couple times through and then just sit around and talk. Setting aside the time to play this game together opened the door to doing more things as a group, as we started to plan full on game days with Catan and Quiplash and Mario Kart, etc. We became really close, and they are still some of my best friends today. I actually met my boyfriend through our Catan nights. This is my favorite memory in college.

Cultivate It

Growing your leisure practices takes time, effort, and commitment. It's important to seek the advice and support of more experienced gardeners. Ask people you admire how they make time for free time. Set up regular times where you and your friends commit to something other than the college party scene. It doesn't have to be a Catan night, if that's not your thing, but don't go it alone.

Weeds have a way of always coming back no matter how hard you try to pull them out. Don't worry. Just recommit to your practices. It's important to be both patient and honest with yourself. You're going to find yourself re-addicted to social media at some point. Acknowledge your failures and move on. Cut yourself a break and try again. Figure out new strategies. Reward yourself when you make progress—even the smallest progress. (But don't reward yourself with the thing you're trying to give up . . . you can't kick a smoking habit with a celebratory cigarette.) Cultivating this garden is a process. It's not a linear improvement. But over time, you'll notice the fruits of your labor.

All relationships are like plants that need regular watering. Your relationship with your sister will only grow and develop with time spent *together*, not just time, but time physically *together*. And that can pose a real challenge when she lives across the country. Don't hesitate to get on a plane when possible. The summer after sophomore year of college, Sofia recalls, "My hometown has a carnival festival each year in July with rides, food, live music, a beer garden. All my friends from high school, even those living long-distance, set aside that weekend to come back and reconnect with old friends." Sofia was able to reconnect with Kylie at the festival that summer, and they begin to rebuild their friendship.

It helps not to go it alone. Find two friends who will commit to cultivating a garden and work together. Maybe find a friend who likes to read but hasn't read for pleasure in a long time. Sofia's friend Sarah is an avid reader of contemporary fiction; she's her go-to whenever Sofia's looking for a new book. And their friendship has deepened over long conversations around good books. You can join a book club or start a book Insta or TikTok or podcast if you want to lean on social media, or you could follow an account of someone you admire for recommendations.

Journal Exercise #14

Write out two or three of the ways you're proud of how you spend your leisure time. You're not bragging. You're coming into yourself.

Congratulate yourself. Catch yourself getting it right. So much of our relationship with ourselves is catching ourselves when we let ourselves down—that leads to self-loathing.

Track your inner emotions, but avoid negative ones. The ones that buzz around like mosquitos. Ignore them and eventually they stop bothering you so much.

Garden Starter Kit

With all the commitments young adults already have, protecting leisure time and making time for friends—and not just by going out to parties or bars—can be tough. Like Babette's Feast, meals are a great place to start. We often approach food as fuel, not as a good to be shared with friends. There are times when you just need a snack, of course, but there's a reason so many societies build their culture around meals together. After Cole landed an internship junior year, he realized he was not consistently hanging out with one group of friends. "I began immediately attempting to get involved in different circles to find my place, but I wanted more than just the same old parties by that point," he says. Cole turned to Sofia and her friend group because he saw that they actually made time for each other. Sofia made sure she ate dinner with her friends. She recalls:

> Freshman year was filled with long dinners at the dining hall every night that lasted hours on end. Dinner was the one time my friends and I could talk, not think about our due dates or dozen club meetings, and recharge. As we passed from freshman to sophomore to junior year, and as people started moving off campus, dining hall dinners became less frequent and our friend group grew smaller, but my core friends and I made sure to still make time for dinner at least once a week. Sometimes our one friend with a meal plan would sneak us into the dining hall, or sometimes we'd go out to dinner. By senior year, we all had apartments and would host each other weekly and prepare the meal together. These dinners were our break from the constant stress of school, internships, job applications. Though it was more work to cook for a group and set

aside a couple of hours in the evenings, I always left our dinners rejuvenated for the week ahead and grateful for my friends.

Don't just schedule your club meetings or intramural practices and gobble dinner down on the go. Schedule dinner with friends. Make sure you sit down. This is an especially important time to put away your phones. Be present to the food you're eating and the friends around the table. You won't suddenly have different habits unless you work at it.

When Sofia finally went to grad school, she and her roommate would invite collections of people who literally had nothing to do with each other and watch an evening emerge out of these encounters. One of their friends was having trouble adjusting to grad school. When he came to one of their dinner parties, he immediately felt like he had found a new community. At one point late in the evening during his first dinner, Sofia asked everyone at the table to share one thing they did that week that they were proud of. Later, she asked everyone to share one failure from their week. These conversations and these dinners allowed friends to be seen and recognized by each other in a way social media could not. Sofia and her roommate literally built a culture of dinner parties, and a new community, out of nothing in grad school. And this skill, once developed, made it such that once Sofia and her husband started having children, they were able to continue to entertain even in the chaos of parenting young children because they already had those habits well-established.

We know this suggestion may sound daunting. No one has time to cook. But you don't have to be a master chef like Babette and prepare a culinary feast. Our students tell us that it's surprisingly easy to pull off your first dinner party. All you need is a few clicks on your iPhone to find an easy recipe. Most recipe apps allow you to download a shopping list directly from the recipe. Don't have time to go grocery shopping before your guests come over? No problem: order your groceries online, and cook while you entertain. Get your friends to help you put the meal together as you have your appetizers. You might burn a couple of meals and have to order out. But that's easy, too.

And buy some candles. Get some wine that doesn't come in a box and use real wine glasses. Maybe dress up a little bit. It's astonishing how much space shapes behavior. If you create an adult and civilized space, people act like adults. If, unlike Sofia's, your dinner group struggles to have easy conversations, make a plan. Be ready with conversation starters (you can actually buy boxes of these or find them online) or trivia games. We've heard of young adults who actually get together and read plays aloud, or play instruments and sing songs without a karaoke machine, or watch films together. If you have trouble scheduling these dinner parties, then start a dinner club where someone hosts once a month. If you live near your friends, organize a progressive dinner party where appetizers are served in one home, main course in another, and dessert in a third. If you have four, then you do a cocktail hour before the appetizer course. You can create a culture of dinner parties among your friend group. You might not start with live turtles like Babette, but it's surprisingly easy to build this habit. Your friends will receive the gift of the first dinner party and want to do the same for you and others.

Decide where you want to start reshaping your leisure time and commit to your first couple of steps. Maybe you want to plan dinners with friends once a week, or leave your phone home when exercising, going out with friends, or reading a fun book. Or maybe you want to start by learning how to play guitar or knit. Set a reminder in your calendar to reread your journal entries from this chapter in one month in order to reassess where you are. Small victories build upon each other to change habits. Living like it matters often comes down to these little choices, repeated until you settle into your new habits.

Section 3: Love

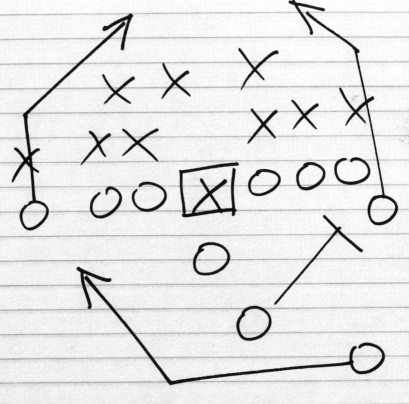

5

Looking for Love

Young adults want live like it matters, but they're not quite sure what that life should look like. We've discussed how they think about work and what they do for leisure. What about the dimension of adult life that outstrips any other? What about love?

For many young adults, there's just no plan for love, and there's not much help either. Parents, teachers, and counselors are at the ready when it comes to helping young people chart the path to a successful career. Sometimes, they're too helpful. But when it comes to love, there are no parents or counselors hovering nearby to help them understand what they're looking for. In fact, adults actively encourage young people to put their love lives on hold until they iron out their professional lives. And yet young adults are attracted to all sorts of people all the time.

While they're often eager to find someone, they're also afraid of what might happen if they do. Will carefully laid career plans fall apart? They might want a partner, but they don't want to be one half of *that* couple—the one that holds hands in public and starts to lose touch with friends because they're always together. They often feel lonely on a campus full of eligible partners who are also frustrated by what's happening (or not happening) in their romantic lives. Maybe partly in response to this loneliness, some will hook up a few times—encounters often fueled by alcohol—only to end up feeling temporarily satisfied, perhaps empty, perhaps worse. Most opt out of romantic relationships. But opting out leaves them feeling like they're missing something essential. Choosing between the romantic chaos of hooking up and the loneliness of opting out leaves young adults with no good options.

Many assume things will somehow get better once they get out in the real world. But if they don't make changes, nothing will change. The students who hook up as undergrads are still hooking up when they're 28. The ones who opt out of romantic life in college don't know how to start a romance in their twenties. And here's the thing—neither group is happy.

Remember Olivia from the leisure chapter? Here's her story of a college romance gone wrong.

PIZZA LOVE

"I could go three years without bad sex," Olivia tells her friend Emma. "But then there'd be no cuddling. The first time you have sex, it's like, hmm that was interesting. I wouldn't mind trying that again. But the first time you cuddle, it's like, wow, this feels amazing. I can finally spoon with a warm body instead of a cold wall. Please don't ever stop holding me." It has been far too long since Olivia has had a good cuddle. So, she approaches Cole, our gamer from the leisure section, in the local college bar because she's had her eye on him for a while. In theory, she's aware of the benefits of casual relationships: "Theoretically, casual relationships are ideal. Theoretically, too, both partners are respectfully sober."

In practice, Olivia and Cole hook up after a night of drinking. "Stop drinking and 90% of college students' sex lives will come to an immediate halt," Olivia thinks. "Theoretically, both partners are detached, and agree on the rules of the casual arrangement. They agree not to catch any feelings or any thoughts about love. . ."

She assumes Cole will check out the next morning, but, unexpectedly, he says they should see each other again. A few days later, Cole comes over. Olivia decides that he's an above average cuddler.

For a while Cole won't take Olivia out in public. "This is the quintessential hook up rule," she realizes. Early into her "relationship" with Cole, she'd spoken to her friend Emma about the fact that Cole wouldn't be seen in public with her. Emma explained: "Everyone knows that once hookups leak outside the bedroom, something changes. Clingy, that's what the women are called, who try to coerce them into public too soon. You know what happens to clingy women? He knows he has you, and so his desires will be quenched, and he will toss you away, like leftover pizza."

One morning, Olivia's stomach growls. She suggests a trip to the Bagel Factory, and Cole agrees. He even buys her breakfast. Olivia's delighted. First cuddling. Now a bagel. In public. "This is what I wanted all along. It looks like this might actually turn into something," she thinks to herself.

They hook up regularly for another month. Then the condom breaks. Olivia goes back and forth between imagining a visit to Planned Parenthood on the one hand and what their child would look like on the other. She decides not to take any chances and invests $49.99 in Plan B. The night before Valentine's Day (a holiday Cole has decided to ignore because, after all, they're not a couple), Olivia texts Cole with a copy of the receipt, who responds "Atta girl" but doesn't offer any money. She decides to drop by the local bar to see if she can catch him, but as she arrives, she notices him leaving with another woman, his arm slung over her shoulder.

Olivia forgoes a dramatic public scene with Cole. Instead, she texts Emma to meet her in the bathroom to help her pull herself together. Olivia feels gut punched, but Emma only adds to the pain by saying, "Don't say I didn't warn you. He knew he had you, and so his desire was quenched, and he tossed you out just like leftover pizza. I told you about this. Pizza love versus real love."

It turns out that Cole was playing according to the rules of pizza love—rules that Olivia "theoretically" agreed to in her own head. And yet, in practice she realized she wanted more. We don't hear Cole's side of the story. But maybe he was just as confused about what he wanted, too. This chapter is going to try to help people like Cole and Olivia understand the difference between what they're settling for and what they're looking for. The next chapter will help them develop new tools they can use to search for something better.

GOING HUNGRY

If pizza love is what's being sold to young adults, it is not surprising that most aren't hungry for it. While "hookup culture" is real, most young adults are actually having less sex than previous generations, and only a minority are engaging in casual sex. In short, while young adults might think that everyone around them is hooking up, most of them are actually opting out of sex entirely. And those who are hooking up are still hungry for something more.

A recent survey by the CDC found that from 2019 to 2021, the percentage of high school students who have had sex decreased from 38% to 30%. Even in college, many students choose to opt out of hookup culture, and those who do participate are not as sexually active as many think. According to the CDC, only 27% of 18 to 29-year-olds nationally had more than one sexual partner in the previous year, and only 8% had four or more partners. These numbers are much lower than what most young people would guess, as seen in another recent study. Psychologist Rich Weissbourd and his team at Harvard's Make Caring Common (MCC) Project, asked students aged 18–25 to guess the percentage of young adults who had hooked up with more than one person in the past year. Their response: between 52 and 54%. Their guess is almost *double* the actual number. A lot of adults—and a lot of young people—think that Gen Z is replete with out-of-control behavior. The truth is the opposite. As the author of one recent study comments, when it comes to sex, most illegal drugs, and crime, young people "are significantly better-behaved than earlier birth cohorts. Moral panics about youth behavior are historical constants, but now they are especially unmoored from reality."

The statistics about what young adults really want in terms of sex might be even more startling. The same MCC survey found that over 70% of respondents reported wishing they had received advice from their parents on romantic relationships. Many wanted advice on "how to have a more mature relationship." With this silence from parents, young adults find models for romance on TikTok and Instagram.

Most young adults desire meaningful relationships and meaningful sex, so it is no wonder that those who do hookup often drink beforehand. Common sense suggests, and psychologist Lisa Damour confirms, that young adults often drink before sex because they are nervous and reluctant to hookup in the first place. Alcohol helps overcome that hesitation (recall the invincible "drunk me" from chapter 3). Contrary to the popular belief that alcohol-fueled sex is at least a good time, recent research at the Indiana University shows that even consensual sex, when under the influence of alcohol, is both less wanted and less enjoyable. In short, far fewer students are hooking up than most people think, and this myth of the hookup culture pressures them into having sex they don't want to have and mixing it with drinking to overcome their reluctance. The result: they are left to deal with the sometimes-devastating consequences.

While the national data about how many young people are actually hooking up shows a downward trend in casual sex, the perception of hookup culture affects social life for young adults in ways that often escape documentation in social science surveys. This is another "social imaginary" (see chapter 4) that is difficult to overcome. You can opt out of pizza love and still be shaped by that culture.

Here's how Jonah describes what going hungry looks like on a college campus:

> Having never done it before, walking up to a girl and asking her out feels physically impossible. The only time I have been able to muster the courage to outwardly flirt with girls is after getting sufficiently drunk at college parties.
>
> Otherwise, the fear of rejection or being judged is too much of a hurdle. I even got a dating app, but didn't get many matches. I got ghosted, and hated the shallowness of it all. Throughout college, I have been so nervous about embarrassing myself or getting rejected that I have failed to seize opportunities right in front of me. Sometimes, it bothers me to even watch movies or shows that portray young, loving relationships or see happy couples on social media, because they remind me how I'm missing out. I put the prospect of being in a relationship on such a pedestal that it has become unapproachable. When genuine opportunities present themselves, I find a reason why that relationship wouldn't work or why it's not the right time. I'm in a prison of my own making.

Or remember Sofia from the work section? Here's how she describes why she decided to opt out by sophomore year of college:

> I feel like ever since I started dating in high school I was surrounded by the message that women should "play hard to get" and that "guys only like the chase." Even texting a guy first seemed like the most desperate and clingy thing you could do. There's a constant pressure to play games and add *spice* to stop men from getting bored of you. I remember when it seemed like every girl at my high school was listening to the

Call Her Daddy podcast that coined the phrases "cheat or be cheated on" and "guys like crazy" in the name of female empowerment. I ended up feeling that hookup culture was the way to go because I thought this carefree, detached persona would be the only way to attract a guy, and then maybe something real would develop later on. The games were exhausting, and I really didn't know another way to go about it, so I kinda stopped hooking up altogether.

So why not just wait till your 30's to pursue romance seriously? If you aren't building your relationship muscles now there's no reason to think that you'll magically get the biceps you want later on. If, at age 27, you realize you want to move away from hanging out at bars and swiping right, and toward a real relationship, you might not know how. If you're a female and 28 and realizing that your fertility has peaked, you might look back and wish things had been different. If you're a guy and 30, you might think the biological clock doesn't affect you, until you find that younger women aren't looking to settle down. They've been trained in the same arena you have and are focused on establishing their careers. You will need something more than hooking up or opting out.

BUILT FOR TRUE LOVE

Confusion about the relationship between love and sex is part of the reason for romantic chaos and loneliness. The typical options aren't fully satisfying because they don't speak to the true love we all desire. Cole was offering pizza love. At first, Olivia accepted this, but then wanted more. In the end, maybe Cole did too. Let's examine the real desire that lies underneath.

Up until now we've been using the term "romantic" love. But "romance" is too tame a word to describe the kind of desire we're talking about. And "love" is too broad a term to work either. After all, we use "love" to describe how we feel about parents, dogs, siblings, or friends. And chocolate, cars, sports teams, or jokes. "Eros" is better to describe the kind of love we mean.

Eros is the Greek root of the English adjective "erotic." At first, we might associate "the erotic" with online porn or strip clubs. That's a mistake. For ancient Greeks, eros wasn't just about sex. Human beings are oriented toward the world "erotically." This is expressed in our desire for romantic relationships, but it also is at the heart of literally *everything* that we do.

Journal Exercise #15

Write about a time when you were working really hard on a math problem or an English paper or a physics experiment or something else.

You've spent hours knocking your head against the wall. You've thrown your hands up in desperation that you'll never get it right. Then, all of a sudden, something clicks and you get the clarity you need to solve the equation, write that thesis sentence, or find the missing ingredient in your experiment.

You've received an insight, and you feel satisfied, at rest. You feel like everything makes sense. Write about what the experience felt like.

Really get yourself back into that moment as you write about it.

Notice how you feel this "aha moment" in your whole body, not just in your brain. This is the erotic dimension of the process of human knowing. Now think about going for a long hike. You've been climbing for hours. You feel the weight of the pack on your back sticking to your sweaty shirt. Your legs feel like logs. But then all of a sudden you come across a clearing and time stops. You no longer feel any weight, but instead feel complete peace. The moment comes as a gift. Or think about when you lose yourself at a concert. The music envelops you and you become one with the crowd. These are erotic moments.

Plato calls eros "a divine madness." Take the madness part first. Eros is born from an encounter with someone or something you find so attractive that you suddenly feel like your world turns upside down. All your carefully laid plans fly out the window. You may feel like you're going crazy. This is why you hear people say "I'm head over heels for him" when they're in love. Erotic love is a disruptor—even of your own sense of who you are and what you thought you wanted.

Think about almost every romantic comedy you've watched. There's usually a hero or heroine who's obsessed with work, or who has given up on love, or who has gotten used to playing the field. She thinks she's in control. She thinks she knows how to manage love. Until "the one" comes along, that is, and the plot line of her life is completely disrupted. Cue the comedy and touching resolution. This plotline is so popular because this is actually what eros does to you—it forces a fundamental reevaluation of who you are and what your life is all about. It feels like your old life is bursting open into a new and abundant kind of existence. People falling in love say corny things like: the flowers smell better, the sun seems brighter, food tastes better. About meeting his future wife, American poet Christian Wiman writes, "When I met Danielle, not only was that gray veil between me and the world ripped aside, colors aching back into things, but all the particulars of the world suddenly seemed in excess of themselves, and thus more truly themselves." When you fall in love, you are broken open and something new is born. This gives you a brief sense of losing control—that's the "falling" part. As you emerge from the fog of that early fall, you find that you're changed. You see yourself and the world differently because you've *been seen*. This is why Plato thought that eros participates in a divine kind of life.

This kind of love is also ecstatic—"ecstasy" comes from two Greek words that mean "standing outside yourself." With eros, we find ourselves moving out of the comfortable places we inhabit, with a desire to come together with the object of our affection. There's clearly a sexual dimension to this. But there's more than that—I want to know the person better so that I can love her more. In turn, I want her to know and love *me* for who I *really am*. To know and be known—to love and be loved—we long for this intimacy. Eros isn't tame; it's a dangerous, wild thrill ride. It involves the body. It also involves the soul and our longing for beauty, meaning, and purpose.

Erotic love is a powerful force in human living. But it's also hard to control. And it's risky. We're creatures built for love, whether we opt out or order in. Both hooking up and opting out attempt to control a mysterious desire that is at the heart of who we are as human beings. On the one hand, reducing eros to sex tries to control one of our deepest desires by turning it into something merely physical and transactional. It's easier to pretend that our desire for love is just about sex. If that were true, all we'd need to do is scratch this itch regularly and we'd be satisfied. On the other hand, we might try to convince ourselves that our desire for love and sex can be repressed and redirected into studying or exercising or working. But both those who hook up and those who opt out are actually reducing the desire for love to the desire for sex. They're just opting for different sides of the same coin.

Instead, eros invites us to look beyond ourselves and into a wider world waiting to be known and loved. Eros builds cathedrals. It writes music that moves our souls. It leads us to create and connect. It makes us more of who we are. It makes us fall in love. But precisely because we're awash in attempts to reduce eros to sex, we shouldn't demand less sex, but ask much more from eros.

HEALING WOUNDS

By the time senior year hit, Cole had learned to stop treating the women in his life like leftover pizza. He met a woman at a party in October and they both experienced an irresistible physical attraction. They drank a little and danced a lot. They found a corner of the living room and had a long conversation about the fact that each had grown up with a close relative with a mental disability. They talked into the night about this. How angry they felt when that person was excluded or made fun of. How when their handicapped relative met their friends, they felt embarrassed and then guilty.

They were each raised with the same wound. It's not an accident that Cole and his now wife both chose careers through which they help young people grow into their potential. Cole is a high school history teacher and coach, and his wife is a child psychologist. Their relationship has healed their own wounds and brought healing to those around them.

Let's look back to the Book of Genesis, where God realizes that it's not good for Adam to be alone. So, he decides to make him a helpmate. He puts Adam into a deep sleep and removes one of his ribs—God creates a wound in Adam. And when Adam sees Eve for the first time, his love for her is inseparable from his wound—she's bone of his bone and flesh of his flesh. Plato's famous dialogue, *The Symposium*, offers a story that also goes deeper into the reality of erotic love.

In Plato's story, humans were originally round beings with four arms, four legs, two heads, and two sets of genitals. They became so powerful and self-sufficient that they threatened the gods. To weaken them, Zeus took his thunderbolt and split them in two. He pulled the skin of each half together like a pouch over the wound he created. Their belly buttons would serve as a constant reminder of their incompleteness and their need. These wounded beings spend the rest of their lives searching for their lost half.

This story reminds us that human beings are radically incomplete. We need each other to do the most basic things. Love is a kind of medicine that heals our incompleteness; our wounds. One of the central experiences of falling in love is feeling like we're meeting our "soul mate." Human beings are each wounded by life in different ways. We all suffer traumas as we grow up, and these traumas are often papered over and even repressed, and yet they manifest themselves in different ways as we grow into adulthood. Love is a cure for a wound that makes you complete.

However, if this is the only dimension of love you recognize—if loving another person is really all about healing yourself and giving you what you need—you might be tempted to a kind of narcissism. You'd only love the other person for what she gives to you. You wouldn't love her because of who she is.

Remember the romantic comedy. He gets into the relationship for selfish reasons, and since the reasons are selfish, they often involve deception. But along the way he falls for her. She discovers the deception, and as a result his original motives. So naturally, the relationship ends for a time, or at least reaches a crisis point. But the hero realizes the error of his ways. He confesses what he's done because he just wants her to be happy. He'll do anything to make that happen, even to the point of giving her up. That's decisive because it means that he's no longer thinking of himself. Now, it's not just about healing his own wounds, but rather it's about caring for her and what's good for her. He's learned his lesson about love. Even while formulaic, romantic comedies get at something real. Ultimately, love takes you out of yourself and attracts you to the goodness of the other.

Love is always a multiplier in these kinds of stories—it is a creative force that brings about something essential and new. Sexuality can be a physical expression of this creative force. It literally brings two lovers together in the most physically intimate way. Sex is a sign of and a way to intimacy that can bring forth new life. It's not the whole of eros, but it's an essential aspect of it. This is why erotic love can never just be pizza love.

Love is a decision to desire the good of the beloved consistently, firmly, resolutely and to work every day to help make that good a reality.

This is easier said than done. Yet, eros breaks the heart open so that it can love the way it's supposed to.

SETTING BOUNDARIES

If eros is a kind of divine madness, and if eros involves this risk of developing a new sense of yourself as you become more intimate with someone else, then figuring out who to let in, how to take the right risks, how to take things slow, when to speed things up, when to trust, how to drop your guard, what to do with misunderstanding, how to stop playing games—all that is extraordinarily difficult. It requires some thought, intention, and courage. It means opening yourself up to new relationships in a way that invites intimacy and trust while keeping you safe.

Becoming intimate with another person is like inviting someone into your home. You have a front porch accessible to everybody. You also have a bedroom upstairs. Sometimes you encounter toxic people who you keep out of your house and even out of your yard. Another time you might invite a new acquaintance up onto your front porch. You might eventually invite him into your living room. Or even to your kitchen for lunch. If so, then he'd be someone you've started to trust. It's a good idea to spend some time in the kitchen.

You start to let yourself become vulnerable with him. You get to know him well enough to have confidence that he can be allowed into your more intimate, personal spaces. This means learning to talk to each other; communicating what you hope for, what you are afraid of, what you think about yourself, what you don't know. Eventually, he'll come to know those private spaces, with their dark corners and cobwebs. But you have to gain the confidence that he won't hurt or judge you while he's learning his way around in there.

Eventually you might invite him into your bedroom. But since that's the most intimate space you have, you have to get to that point gradually and be intentional about what you're doing. Having gotten to know him on an intellectual and emotional level, and having established trust between the two of you, you might be ready to invite him to cross that threshold. You have to reach a point where you're fairly certain that he wants to be there for the right reasons—he is there because he wants to know and love you more deeply.

Trust is always earned. And it's always a two-way street. This mutuality and growing sense of faith in each other has to be real. If you're asking your friend into the kitchen, and he's not letting you off his front porch, you've got yourself a problem.

In "Pizza Love," Olivia gets this process of intimacy backwards; she invites Cole into her bedroom to get him to sit down at her kitchen table. She really just wanted a bagel and a cuddle. If eating a bagel together at the kitchen table doesn't work out the way she hopes, she can let Cole leave her house without much harm to either of them. None of that is true with hooking up. That's a high-risk proposition with potentially devastating consequences. At the end of the story, she's hurt because Cole acted like a jerk. But she's also hurt because she started in the wrong room, so she didn't give herself a chance to figure out whether she really wanted to get closer to him in the first place; she didn't give herself enough time—at a distance—to figure out what kind of guy he was. Maybe she didn't need to start in the bedroom to get Cole into the kitchen. She could have begun more safely—emotionally and physically—and just offered him a bagel instead. If she'd done that, maybe she would have recognized some warning signs before she gave herself over to the relationship in ways he didn't deserve.

It starts with boundaries. We all have to navigate them; to figure out who to keep out and who to let in. We can think about the house metaphor as an exercise in healthy boundaries. Keeping yourself—your identity—intact means maintaining healthy boundaries with those around you. One kind of boundary problem involves not knowing what room you should start in and where you should end. If you don't really know who you are and where you stop and start, then you're tempted to invite all sorts of people and things into your life too fast. For example, you might mistakenly share too much information online too quickly.

But there's another kind of boundary problem where your house is a fortress. Maybe you've been hurt by a girlfriend. Or you've seen your parents tear each other up in a divorce. Or maybe you're afraid of not meeting your career goals, so at campus parties you avoid the guy you're attracted to. If you don't take a risk, you are locking your doors and turning your house into a prison. There is a different way to pursue your romantic life like it matters. The next chapter shows how.

6

Finding Love

As we learned in the last chapter, many young adults opt out of both meaningless hook-ups and quasi-marital relationships. At the end of the day, they really want to remain optimistic about romance. They want to find love, even if they get freaked out by the search. Here's Cole, trying as best he can to put a good spin on the college dating landscape: "If there ever was a time to just be free and adventurous, then it is definitely college. Random hook-ups rarely lead to actual connection, but it's not impossible to find love." But couldn't it be easier, less taxing, and more fun? Definitely. Here's how.

> **Journal Exercise #16**
> Write about a crush you've had.
> • What drew you to the person?
> • Why did it never become a relationship?
> • What is it about a crush that's so hard to approach?

Junior year, Olivia ends up in a class that includes a dating assignment. The professor adapted this assignment from Dr. Kerry Cronin at Boston College, known across the country as "the dating doctor." Maybe this sounds really weird, but lots of students have done it and found out that it works. We invite you to do it, too.

The assignment teaches students that casual dating can be just that: casual. Not casual sex. Casual dating. You can give casual dating a try. And if it doesn't work out, there's no harm, no foul. But to say that this dating is casual does not mean it happens spontaneously. It's intentional. It's designed to train you to find someone worth dating in a real way. Think of it like the "summer internship" of your job search, as it prepares you for real relationships. Dating is a safe way to invite someone into your house.

There is nothing threatening about the assignment. It restricts physical contact to a possible brief "A-frame" hug. The date shouldn't take longer than about 90 minutes and should happen in a public place. No alcohol is allowed. The person who asks out pays the bill. In order to avoid unnecessary drama, only tell two friends about this date. And no texting during the date . . . phones off or on "do not disturb."

This assignment helps students rewrite the social script currently in play across campuses nationwide. Sure, some students try it once and never do it again. But others give it a go, and it transforms the way they walk through college. The assignment also gives some students the courage to turn a regular hookup arrangement into an actual healthy relationship.

A PLAYBOOK FOR DATING
Phase 1: Try It

Here's one student's reflection about an experience with the initial ask:

> My heart was beating out of my chest as I started walking to his dorm. I felt my hands start to sweat and get clammy. I was confused as to why I was so nervous to see him; we've been friends since the beginning of the school year and I've been to his dorm room so many times. I nervously walked into the building and reluctantly moved towards his room. As I lifted my hand to knock on his door, I felt my arm start to shake. It took me a few seconds, but I finally worked up enough courage to knock. I stood there waiting for him to open the door, questioning the decision I made to walk over there. As I heard the door open, my heart sank into my stomach, and I immediately felt a rush of butterflies swarming inside. I wanted to run away, but instead I smiled and said "hi" when he saw me.

Almost without exception, students share these feelings of awkwardness (or even abject terror), especially during "the ask." They talk about sweaty palms, churning stomachs, frozen vocal cords. Olivia walked to her date's dorm room four times before actually having the courage to knock on the door to ask him out.

Students talk about how much more difficult it is to ask someone out in person instead of over text, how much more courage it takes to actually have to face potential rejection. But once given a chance to reflect on their anxieties during the initial ask, they realize that the ask was much easier in retrospect than it had initially seemed. Sure, some students get rejected, and rejection sucks. But in every other area of life, young people are taught to get back up on the horse and keep riding. You can be sure that if you go into sales or investing, you'll make lots of asks that could end in a "no." Why not in romance? While texting seems like the easier way to ask someone out on a date, think about how many times you've received a text and stared at it, trying to decipher the words. An in-person ask is so much easier to interpret. And harder to reject.

It's also so much more human.

Once on the date, many students report feelings of awkwardness and discomfort, and a difficulty navigating those inevitable pauses in conversation. These feelings are often heightened when they're in the dreaded "friend zone" with the person they asked out. One student reflects that the dating assignment forced him to escape the hookup culture, but only to an extent: "even on a real date, I still felt like hookup culture was interfering because both of us were so used to not dating that it left us feeling awkward and unsure." But maybe it's just those moments of awkwardness that build up one's relationship muscles. You gain the confidence to ask someone out for a coffee date by, well, asking someone out for coffee. You get the skills you need to approach someone you are interested in—by approaching someone you're interested in. And you'll get better and better at it the more you try.

It's comfortable to gravitate toward Snapchat, Instagram, DM, and texting. The options of leaving a conversation at any point, carefully crafting a response, or worse, asking others for input before writing back are always on the table. But none of this "connectedness" leads to easy, free-flowing, enjoyable, or meaningful direct conversations. This is why phones should be banned during the date. And as one student remarked, "When you're texting with a girl, you're basically texting her whole friend group." Live conversations aren't recorded.

If you find that first date over coffee too awkward, then the next time you could try asking another guy out for a walk in a public setting. Sometimes, doing an activity together instead of sitting and staring at each other over a latte is less intimidating. But the first date can't be anything too complicated. It shouldn't be set up to take too long. It should just be an opportunity to be casual outside the bedroom.

And the more casual dates you go on, the more casual they actually become. It's like running. The first few times, you feel like you might die. But once running becomes a habit, you wake up, throw on your shoes and head out the door. Casual dating can be like that, too. You get to know lots of guys in a casual setting. Like running, you've got a purpose in mind. But like running, you don't put too much stock in any one run. You're getting to know people on the front porch, where they belong at that stage of intimacy.

Why is this process so full of anxiety? We have a sense when we ask someone out something really essential is at stake—our heart's longings. If she rejects my invitation, isn't she rejecting *me*? If I ask someone out, aren't I admitting that I find him attractive? How do I put myself out there like that? If he accepts my invitation, what comes next? Of course this is very new. It's different. Young adults *just don't do things this way*. But that's no reason to accept the status quo.

It's important, then, to realize that for the people you ask out, your invitation may seem to come from out of the blue; they might not know what to make of it initially. What you intend to be a casual date with no strings attached might be fraught with all kinds of other associations for them that you didn't imply. For instance, Jonah completed the dating assignment in his freshman year. He really enjoyed that first date, so he wanted to date some more. He asked a few young women out. He reported that some of them were freaked out. "What does it mean that you're asking me to dinner?" they'd ask. "Are you saying you want to be exclusive? I barely know you." Behind these questions there were others: "What kind of guy is this? Should I take this guy up on his invitation or be worried about his intentions?" It's instructive that one of the young women in Jonah's friend group became his long-term girlfriend. The person he eventually found was someone who knew him well enough to trust his motives when he asked her out on a first date.

Asking someone on a date doesn't mean cold calling a stranger, like some creepy telemarketer trolling for a vulnerable buyer. More often than not, it means asking someone out with whom you've already interacted for a while—whether in a class or a club or hanging out with friends. But this last one can be tricky. Mustering up the courage to pull someone out of the "friend zone" is tough. You might fear what your mutual friends will think. You might worry what will happen if things go south. Recognize that fear and set it aside. The whole point of starting with casual dates is that there isn't the same heartache if it doesn't work than if you start with physical intimacy. And, on the flip side, you don't want to regret a lost opportunity.

Finally, of course, this is risky; you might get shot down, or you might even get hurt. But what's happening with romance isn't working for young adults. It hurts many people in much more scarring ways than dashed hopes or humbled pride. We need a different model. As scary as asking someone out might be, the current alternatives of hooking up or opting out are worse.

Consider whether the person you've had your eye on for the last few months is worth the risk. Having completed the dating assignment, Sofia changed her dating practices during college:

> During the first week of freshman year, I met a boy named Sam in a dorm room where a bunch of my friends were hanging out. I didn't see him again until the first week of my sophomore year. I was in the quad, and he recognized me and said "hello." After that we kept running into each other around campus, and I always made it a point to say hello. He at times would stop and chat with me. This went on for 2–3 weeks. He then asked me as his date to one of his frat functions, and we had a ton of fun (but all PG). The next week after my night class I asked if he wanted to get ice cream. It lasted about an hour, and it was fun! He made me laugh and smile in a way that watching Netflix with friends never could (not that I don't love my girlfriends, but they don't make me giddy quite like he does). I didn't instantly fall in love, but I enjoyed getting to know him better. After ice cream we've gotten lunch on campus a handful of times. At this point we've been casually dating for about 4–5 weeks.

If you're asking a friend out, you'll have to clarify that you'd like to explore a new possibility, but that if it doesn't work out that you'll be fine to remain friends. Brooke and her now-husband were part of the same friend group for about a year when she was in her twenties before Brooke finally mustered up the courage to make a move. One night at the end of a party, she said to him, "I need to talk to you." "Why don't we go for Chinese food tomorrow night?" he responded. Once at the table, Brooke told him, "I'm interested in you." Things didn't go so well at first, since he *totally* ignored what she said and asked her about the party the night before. She went to the bathroom at one point to give herself a pep talk, and somehow managed to keep her composure throughout dinner. At the end, in a surprising twist, he said, "So when are we going to go out again?" And, as they say, the rest is history.

Once you go out with someone two or three times, and you're ready to start to focus on one person, you've got to have the courage to define the relationship.

Journal Exercise #17

After having completed your dating assignment, sit down and write in your journal about what worked and what didn't go so well.
• What was most challenging about the experience?
• What did you find yourself enjoying?
• Was it a difficult muscle to flex?
• Writing down the details will help clarify your own desires for you.

Phase 2: Name It

DTR. Define The Relationship. That's the talk two people have when one of them has the courage to ask the other what the heck they've been doing these past several weeks or months. Today's dating culture is confusing in this regard. Listening to young adults correct each other about how one moves from "talking" to "hanging" to becoming "official"—or are they just in a "situationship"—makes it painfully obvious that there are no real markers in today's dating world other than posting a photo on Instagram (and think about how much thought goes into whether or not to post that photo). And what's a "thing," anyway? One student admits that most young adults don't want to commit to a relationship. Instead, "Most people are in this 'talking' stage where they do not have to define their relationship. Perhaps they fear rejection or feel too much pressure to be faithful." So how does the "talking" stage turn into something more defined? It's unclear. Here's Olivia:

> I know people who are "exclusive" (meaning they can't hook up with other people), but they refuse to refer to each other as boyfriend or girlfriend. They're not "allowed" to hook up with other people, but they still

refuse to say that they're 'dating.' There's literally no difference between dating and being exclusive except their refusal to label it.

And then there's social media, which adds another level of anxiety: "Being 'insta-official' is often a big step in people's relationship. This makes them official because now everyone can see that they're "together."

So, is the resistance to Define The Relationship actually Fear Of Missing Out? One student admits, "I'm afraid that if I get in a relationship, I'll be missing out on someone better." FOMO plagues students in all aspects of their lives, not just dating. Today's Tinder mentality turns potential partners into commodities and makes us always on the lookout for the best buy, or to trade up. This is anti-eros all the way.

Once you've dated someone casually for a couple of weeks, what does it mean to go to the next step? You may want to go on longer dates, such as dinner and a movie, or a long hike. Clearly state your intentions. Agree to focus on each other in this way. This can go on for months. Think of yourself at the kitchen table. You can spend a lot of time there.

The dates you go on together will change as you grow closer. It's not just that the dates will get longer. It's that as you learn about the other person, you learn what he loves, what he's good at. You meet the people in his life. You'll meet his best friend. He loves baseball, so you'll go to a ball game, even though you've never had the slightest interest in the sport.

How do you know whether to invite the person you're starting to date off the front porch of your life, into the kitchen, and maybe upstairs? There's no easy recipe or formula. You can't expect certainty when you try to answer a question like that. That's part of the reason love is so risky. Here's another wrinkle: many of the traditional ways of proceeding no longer seem to apply.

Some obvious signs are still in place, though: you find your date attractive; he makes you laugh; he handles his emotions well; she wants to have kids eventually and so do you; she's smart and compelling; your values align; you're a better person when she's around. But you should also pay attention to manners. Not the usual sense of "manners," as though you pick the guy who knows which salad fork to use or the one who will open the car door for you. But "manners" as in: habits of behavior that show people you care about them. Does your date make you uncomfortable in an already anxious situation? Does your date take an opportunity to make fun of you or belittle you? Does your date play games over text? Or share too much about what happened on your date with her friends? Or does your date think about how his actions might make you feel? Does she put her phone away over dinner to look at you and pay attention to what you have to say? Does he listen—really listen—to what you're saying and try to understand what you mean?

Once you're ready to bring your guard down and let this person really get to know who you are, and you're ready to get to know this other person intimately, then you're ready to transition to a serious relationship. This is the point at which you have to think about whether you're ready to utter the words, "I love you." You signal that your heart knows it can be broken. When you say those words, everything changes, and the stakes go way up. Here, the emotional work of dating begins to really take shape. Here, you're building actual relationship muscles that you'll take with you no matter where you end up with this person. Here, you take on each other's joys and sorrows. But does that mean that even after you say the three little words that this suddenly becomes a quasi-marital relationship? Absolutely not.

Phase 3: Let It Breathe

Changing the social script to include casual dating is a great start, but what about the concerns that a relationship means trading in your group of friends for one person who absorbs all your free time? Why does being "serious" have to entail spending half of your nights in someone else's bed? Remember that boundaries can go wrong in two ways: too little and too much. If your relationship is closed in on itself too tightly, you'll smother it. And each other.

One student admits that "during an already-stressful time in a young adult's life, the added pressure to maintain and cultivate a longstanding, fruitful relationship can be taxing." Relationships needn't become all-absorbing. In fact, if exclusive dating entails ignoring your friends, you're setting yourself up for a suffocating marriage. American poet Christian Wiman writes, "The great paradox of love, and not just romantic love, is that a closer focus may go hand in hand with a broadened scope. 'To turn from everything to one face,' writes Elizabeth Bowen, 'is to find oneself face to face with everything.'" So, moving from casual dating to a serious relationship should never entail ditching your friends. In fact, if it does, this is a warning sign that this relationship isn't going to go the distance.

In a serious relationship, you want to come to know the person as she truly is, and you want to let that person in to get to know you without any of the masks you wear. This is scary. You may find that, after you've invested significant time and emotional energy in someone, she is not genuinely willing to respect your boundaries or to reciprocate the same kind of investment in you. It's important to realize that even after months or years of serious dating, there is still time to walk away. You don't have to think of the time and energy and love invested as simply lost, as long as you've grown to be a better, more loving, more perceptive person in the process.

But opening yourself up this way—slowly and carefully—is worth the risk, because when you succeed, it's so liberating. Here, you are actually preparing yourself for the challenges and joys of a happy lifelong partnership.

Phase 4: Support It

Once young people begin to develop the practice of casual dating, many become dating ambassadors. Your own dating successes will encourage others to do the same. You'll surround yourself with a group of people that are choosing something different, and it becomes a possibility for others. Remember when some people started bringing their own reusable water bottles places so as not to use disposable plastic? This used to be outside the norm. Now everyone is doing it. Each of these changes begins with just a few people wanting to change their environment.

Maybe you met a couple who gave you a glimpse into what a happy marriage and family could look like. You begin to desire a marriage like that one. The same happens with healthy dating. If you see other people doing it well, you start to want to do the same. So you do. And then you become a concrete model of that for others. In

> **Journal Exercise #18**
> Think about relationships you've seen.
> • What were the positive aspects you want to emulate?
> • Negative aspects to keep at bay?
> • What relationships serve as models for you going forward? Why?
> • What specific things have you learned from toxic relationships? Name them.

the dating realm, as in all of the important parts of your life, you have to surround yourself with people who will understand and support the kinds of choices you want to make. Healthy casual dating works best when it is nurtured by a wide web of healthy friendships. It takes just a few friends to get this started.

Phase 5: Plan For It

We began this chapter by noting that our students tend to plan for everything except love. Perhaps a little planning is called for in the dating world. When you start to get more serious, take the time to have a plan for your date that includes a strategy for things like the physical intimacy you're comfortable with at this point in your relationship, how you're going to handle the "who pays" question, and what you're willing to share now. Make strategies for things like how you respond if you're invited back into the dorm room, how much you'll allow yourself to drink, what you're going to do if the date goes bad (extra cash, Uber, friends' contact information), and what your limits are if the date goes better than expected. You want a plan that keeps you healthy and that changes as things in the relationship change. And a plan that allows you to gradually achieve physical and emotional intimacy.

WHEN THINGS GO OFF TRACK

You might have arrived at the end of these five phases and thought, "If only it were so easy." There is no way to protect yourself from heartbreak. No way to anticipate the breakup that will leave you feeling annihilated. And five rejections in a row for a coffee date is tough to stomach. As C. S. Lewis recognizes:

> To love at all is to be vulnerable. Love anything and your heart will be wrung and possibly broken. If you want to make sure of keeping it intact you must give it to no one, not even an animal. Wrap it carefully round with hobbies and little luxuries; avoid all entanglements. Lock it up safe in the casket or coffin of your selfishness. But in that casket, safe, dark, motionless, airless, it will change. It will not be broken; it will become unbreakable, impenetrable, irredeemable. To love is to be vulnerable.

This chapter has tried to sketch out a healthy plan that guides you through this rough terrain in a humane way. When you date casually you cast a wide net.

Remember that, just as the initial ask is ideally to be done in person, so should the breakup be. We hear too many awful stories about being "ghosted." It's no wonder students are hesitant to open themselves up to relationships when one day the person could just disappear from their lives, from their screens, with no prior notice. If you want to end the relationship, exit it as gracefully and forthrightly as you entered. There are plenty of ways to let someone down in a way that enables him to maintain his integrity, in a way that crushes him a little less. Be clear but be gentle. And if you're on the receiving end, pick up the pieces, pull yourself together and keep casting your net.

You're worth it.

THE GOALS OF THE PLAN

Different people are called to different ways of life, and different people have different callings at different times of their lives. Marriage isn't necessarily for everyone. But if statistics are to be believed, most of you plan to get married and start families . . . eventually.

Further, each of you is an individual and not a statistic. If there's one consistent message in this book—whether it's about your work, or your friendships, or your relationship with yourself—it's having a good playbook doesn't tell you how the actual gameplay will unfold. Your path is uniquely your own, and you have to find it.

Statistics do reveal what kinds of choices your peers typically make when they get older: most say they want to get married; and most college graduates will get married, and most will stay married. According to a Pew Research study, six out of every seven adults who have not been married say they want to get married. In 2015, among adults ages 25 and older, 65% of people with a four-year college degree were married. Finally, college educated women who married twenty years ago have an 8 in 10 chance of still being married. It might seem like more and more people are shying away from thinking about how to create their own families. But just as we learned that hooking up is much less common than you might have initially thought, the rumors about the death of marriage have been greatly exaggerated.

Erotic love is a dynamic process that carries us out of our narrow narcissism into an encounter with another person. It's not a movement from selfishness to a cold altruism. It's a movement from self-enclosure to a decision to care for the good of the person you love the most. This movement fundamentally changes us and makes us more human. We are built for relationships. It's written into the fabric of who we are. Olivia became more human, more *uniquely her*, as she entered more deeply into her relationships as friend, as student, as sister, as wife, as mother. There is no better way to uncover who she truly is. Cole became more human as he learned to love his wife and children, his students, athletes, and friends better. As we give ourselves over to another in love, we become more authentically whom we were meant to be.

And there's more. This movement into love always issues in abundance; it moves beyond the narrow self to new ways of being. Love is fertile. It blossoms in unexpected ways. That new relationship can heal a deeply held wound, it can give hope to a friend who has only witnessed broken relationships, it can give you the courage to take that career risk. Olivia's next boyfriend after Cole made her more ambitious, and she learned to not accept initial rejections as the final word. She also came to believe in herself more because he believed in her. The fruits of this relationship are still with her even though the guy isn't. This kind of love is fertile. Socially. Culturally. But physically too. It's what creates new life. Eros is a multiplier. Trust it. Hope in it. Be brave for it.

FOR A NEW BEGINNING

In out-of-the-way places of the heart,
    Where your thoughts never think to wander,
This beginning has been quietly forming,
    Waiting until you were ready to emerge.

For a long time it has watched your desire,
    Feeling the emptiness growing inside you,
Noticing how you willed yourself on,
    Still unable to leave what you had outgrown.

It watched you play with the seduction of safety
    And the gray promises that sameness whispered,
Heard the waves of turmoil rise and relent,
    Wondered would you always live like this.

Then the delight, when your courage kindled,
    And out you stepped onto new ground,
Your eyes young again with energy and dream,
    A path of plenitude opening before you.

Though your destination is not yet clear
    You can trust the promise of this opening;
Unfurl yourself into the grace of beginning
    That is at one with your life's desire.

Awaken your spirit to adventure;
    Hold nothing back, learn to find ease in risk;
Soon you will home in a new rhythm,
    For your soul senses the world that awaits you.

John O'Donohue

Conclusion

A New Beginning

Having come to the end of the book, you might wonder what happened to students like Brooke, Sofia, Cole, and Jonah. The characters in this book are composites of students we've taught over the years who have graduated and built successful professional and personal lives. They took our classes and followed our advice. This last chapter is woven together with words from these graduates. It offers models of what becoming a flourishing adult actually looks like. Like Brooke and Cole, you can follow in their footsteps.

The thing about the achievement trap is that it never stops. Remember the introduction, that marathon Jonah was stuck in? It follows you after graduation if you choose to run it. The temptation to compare yourself to your peers never ends. With social media at the ready, showing us how great everyone else's lives are, it's hard to catch a break. Here's Jonah, reflecting back on life before graduation:

> I used to view happiness as a job and constantly compare myself to others. How is everyone else creating their happiness? What am I missing that they have? What are they missing that I have? Am I doing better than them in the areas in which we overlap? If happiness is a race to be won, nothing is enough. Time never stops moving and the finish line keeps plunging further into the future. It keeps moving year after year, seemingly faster and faster, setting new expectations for the chasers.

In high school, it was getting into an elite university. In college, it was scoring a prestigious full-time job. In five years, it will be getting engaged to my "soul mate," and in ten it will be acting like a great parent to the kids I had with said soulmate. When will it ever be enough?

This book has helped you begin to cultivate the habits to rise above the long sort, to step out of the race and build your own life, the one that works *for you*. Cultivating these habits isn't a linear development. It happens in fits and starts. But small changes now can make a world of difference years from now. Young adults like you are plagued by choice paralysis, a fear of failure, and a reluctance to take risks, both professional and personal.

We return to Jonah and Olivia, who stood in your shoes, but who ultimately chose to take those professional and personal risks, who took the plunge and reaped rich rewards.

RISKING WORK

Here's Jonah, recounting his college experience and his first years out:

Growing up, a loved one used to give well-intentioned advice that "every day can't be a day at Disney World." Without fail, I'd counter each time: "Why not?"

Fast-forward to the present and that sentiment remains unchanged. Leaving aside my distaste for amusement parks, every day *is* a day at Disney World.

Is it because my employment's equal parts philanthropic, stimulating, and lucrative? Or because I live in a converted 19th century drawing room with eighteen-foot ceilings and drive a German coupe? Or perhaps because I enjoy good health and exercise as much as English cigarettes and dry Hendrick's martinis (don't forget the lemon twist)?

In a word, "no." I love life not due to what I get out of it, but due to what I put into it. My journey to this realization, and unpacking what it means, takes us back a decade.

I entered college hungry, on a mission to rub my intelligence in the face of having been denied admission to each of my top school choices. Armed with a semester's worth of Advanced Placement credits, I leveraged a uniquely flexible schedule to take graduate level courses in philosophy and political science. Except for a B in Italian—*I'm not bitter, I'm not bitter, I'm not bitter*—my scores were perfect across the board.

I was also miserable. Beneath a façade of academic confidence and indifference for everything else, inside I was crippled by social anxiety and depression. When I wasn't in pain from mental unhealth or the side effects of alcohol and drug binges, I was numb under a deluge of prescribed pharmaceuticals.

No matter, so I thought—*I was successful.* Graduated top of my class. Admitted to one of the country's best law schools. Wined and dined by New York City's prestigious law firms. Offered a coveted spot in the nation's preeminent real estate legal department. An apartment in the well-heeled West Village. It didn't matter that my life was built on someone else's value system.

Until it did.

It all blew up within a couple weeks. I was experiencing suicidal ideation daily. My life had gone so far in the wrong direction that only a hard reset could course-correct. I quit my job and ended a long-term relationship in quick succession.

People said I'd never get back on track. The decisions I made in those few weeks turned out to be the best I ever made.

The next year-and-a-half was formative. I tried to start a real estate investment company and failed. However, in doing so I learned the business side of the industry and identified an emerging market in upstate New York to which I moved. I rented the cheapest month-to-month apartment I could find and resisted buying a car, using the money I saved to make business connections traveling and over dinner. I worked multiple full-time jobs, practicing law during the day and consulting at night.

The knowledge I accumulated from my unique mix of legal and business experience impressed a business connection. A cold LinkedIn message and several months of interviews later, I was offered an opportunity that reflects *my* value-system—General Counsel of a mission-driven affordable housing development company. As lead attorney for over $750M in development, I'm using my skills to change the world for the better. My colleagues are sharp and kind. The role is challenging and pays well. For the first time in longer than is easy to admit. . .I'm happy.

I love my job, but it's not why I love my life. I'm happy because the process that brought me to my current position is something that will always be mine. Any undesired outcome is either a function of the process I control, or a deviation that will pass with time. Controlling what I give, which in turn determines what I get, is as simple as choosing to live a life that excites me every morning and for which I'm grateful every night.

No matter who you are, that choice can be yours too. It's as simple as making it.

It took a lot of courage for Jonah to walk away from one of the most lucrative law firms in the country. He didn't know whether he would ultimately succeed in his new ventures, and at first, in fact, he failed. He drew from his savings when leaving the firm, and he moved back in with his parents. Sure, it wasn't glorious for a while, and of course his first venture didn't quite pan out. But it only took a couple of years for him to end up professionally fulfilled. And he's only 30.

We know because we saw it happen. We saw the courage that it took to make that career change, to not settle for less than his dream, even while not knowing along the way how his dream would actually take shape concretely in real life.

Don't sell yourself short in your professional life. Your dreams are worth it. And so are you.

RISKING FOR LOVE

Now let's get to know what happened to Olivia after she graduated. She recalls how she took the leap for a new relationship, knowing that it could blow up in her face, but having the courage to leap just the same.

We met freshman year of college, shortly after Orientation, and I could tell pretty quickly that this was someone I wanted to spend time with. And spend time we did . . . at the library, getting lunch, and walking back to our dorm after class together. It's been over ten years since that September, and while the memories aren't as sharp, I remember loving any time I spent with Ryan. He is smart, witty, gentle, and kind. One night we went on a walk around campus as a study break, making our way to an empty basketball court, and laid down to stargaze. I asked him if he believed in God, or anything bigger than us. He asked me if I thought we were pawns in an alien video game. I laughed. He made me think *and* made me laugh, and that felt like a rare combination. We had a falling out a few months later . . . things between us felt too intimate to call it a friendship, and neither of us had the courage to call it what it was. The falling out felt like a breakup, and I vowed never to speak to him again. I kept my distance the next three years, and I thought after graduation I'd never see him again.

While he moved to New York City, I went to graduate school then took a teaching job in San Diego. My roommate from college lived on the East Coast, and I would visit her once a year around her birthday. At a party four years after graduation, I landed in Providence, Rhode Island, and hopped in an Uber.

Claire called me. "Ryan's going to be here!"

I was stunned; I didn't know he had moved out of NYC.

"I'm sorry," she continued, "I know we're supposed to hate him, but I'm new to the city and ran into him and I need friends!" I sighed. "Thankfully I just got my hair done, and our falling out was ages ago . . . I'm fine. . ." I finally said.

I walked into the party, we made eye contact, and I was surprised when he approached me quickly and said hello, asking me how I was doing. The party went late into the night, and I found myself slipping into conversation with him. Many hours and several drinks later, one of us brought up freshman year. We agreed neither of us handled it well, and I even said, "That never really felt like just a friendship." He fascinated me, just as he had all those years ago, and I left that visit thinking about him. But I lived across the country, and why would it be worth risking anything eight years later? We both had had serious relationships in college, and mine ended by being dumped by the man I thought I'd marry. It was painful enough to oscillate between not ever wanting to be in a relationship again and then clinging to a new relationship, doing everything to make it work instead of recognizing it wasn't healthy. I absolutely didn't feel quite like putting myself out there for someone who didn't really seem like a perfect fit on paper. The Ryan I knew in college was a self-proclaimed atheist, had a tense relationship with his brother, and wanted to work 80 hours a week for an investment bank. Not exactly what I pictured when I thought of my perfect match. I loved books and wanted to be a teacher or work in college student life. I never wanted to live in a city or let work rule my life. The thought of Ryan was alluring, sure, but I figured I was just harboring an old crush.

Over the years, when I'd go back and visit my college friends, I'd try to find a way to invite him out with us. He always made it a fun night, and slowly Ryan revealed a different narrative of his life—he had done the investment banking thing, and it had sucked the life out of him. He couldn't stand the idea of making rich people richer and wanted to find meaning in work. He had moved to Providence to enjoy a slower pace of life. The two of us would end up standing at the bar, as I peppered him with questions about why he left his lucrative job in New York, why he started meditating, why he decided to give up alcohol for months at a time (he called this my "Interrogation"). After those nights out, I'd go home with Claire and say, "Someone *has* to date Ryan!" She would exclaim back, "Why don't you just date him!" "He's not the guy for me," I'd rationalize. "We don't see life the same way, and I live halfway across the country! It wouldn't work."

Over a year after that first reunion, I was back in Providence for a college friend's wedding. I had left San Diego and moved home to the Midwest, working a job I didn't love but finding myself in a good groove being closer to family and friends, starting therapy, and getting a puppy. I felt like myself for the first time in a long time, and I wasn't even phased that I didn't have a plus one to this wedding. A group of us grabbed drinks in the city, and I jokingly said, "I'm going to invite Ryan." It might have even taken some liquid courage to grab my friend's phone and dial his number (I know, a bit of a cop out). "Your presence is requested at the beer garden near Claire's!" I said. He showed up a little while later, and it was obvious the energy between us had shifted. I felt like we honed in on each other the entire evening . . . we walked through the city streets with our friends to the next bar and he and I hung back to walk alone. He confided in me why he had wanted to quit his private equity job and find something more fulfilling. I told him that I was working on building a better relationship with my parents. "Are you free for lunch tomorrow?" he finally asked. I said "yes," and on a whirlwind weekend we went to lunch the day before the wedding, and dinner the day after. I learned he and his brother healed a five-year rift and were now closer than ever. He loved reading books about Buddhism. He was considering leaving his finance career altogether. He decided to learn to surf and described the sublime experience of being out on the ocean. Conversation flowed naturally, we were both eager to learn about each other, to fill in those gaps we created a decade prior.

When it was over, I got back on a plane and flew home to the Midwest, back to my comfortable life. For days, I was telling my friends, "You'll never believe it! I reconnected with my freshman year crush and we kissed! It was amazing!" I chalked it up to a funny story, a magical weekend, and nothing more for a couple weeks. But we kept talking.

He would text, and eventually, call. I thought I'd date someone closer to home, but he was almost 700 miles away. I kept telling myself it wasn't going to go anywhere, but we kept making every effort to see each other.

Within a few months, I knew this was the real deal. He was better than the story I made up for myself in my mind about what a perfect partner would look like. He was interested in *me* in all my uniqueness, and he showed through his actions he was committed—flying across the country to meet my friends, hanging out with my family, inviting me to meet his parents. We read books together, we both liked walking around the city, and he bonded with my dog.

Six months in, he visited my family for a week and worked late into the evening. While the rest of us were going on an evening walk, he was slouched over his laptop. When I brought him dinner, he made one of many off-hand comments about needing to leave his job. I looked at him, "Well, when are you going to do it?" He balked. We talked through his fears—that all those years of hard work and long hours in banking would be for nothing, that people would see him as a failure, that my parents would think he was crazy. We also elevated all the opportunities that could come from a move like this—the chance to reset, to surf more, to search for a job that was meaningful and fulfilling. He finally said, "I guess you can always make more money, but you can never make more time." He didn't want to be working during a family vacation anymore.

While still doing long distance, Ryan and I decided to both look for jobs we were more passionate about in a new city together. Ryan left his job in finance and sought out a fresh profession. I ended up applying for and getting a job at our alma mater working with college students in the career center. It wasn't a promotion. In fact, it was a lateral move, and it meant leaving my dear friends and the amazing community I had built in the Midwest. When I told one friend I was moving to where Ryan was, she said, "Why isn't he moving for you? I thought you were all about female empowerment!" Even though the decision was hard, and people thought it was too soon, and I wasn't sure I would love the job, I knew that this relationship was more important than pursuing a promotion. I knew Ryan was life-partner material, and that our budding love was worth the leap of faith.

Ryan and I didn't have the easiest road to each other; it was marked with missteps and heartbreak and bad jobs and difficult moves. And many things remain imperfect and unknown. Are either of us in our "forever jobs"? Probably not. Has he found the perfect place to pivot in his career? Certainly not. But we're hammering it out together, and learning to place what we both value at the center of that togetherness. We're not willing to compromise love or leisure for the sake of employment, and that comes with its consequences. What keeps us going is that we were led back to each other, that we both feel a sense of purpose together, and that we get to choose our relationship every single day.

Olivia and Ryan learned how to take risks for each other and their happiness. They don't have their lives worked out yet, but they're taking a chance on their future happiness together and hammering out how their professional lives will work into that happiness. Reflecting back, Olivia finds, "If my journey through my last 28 years of life has taught me anything, it is that to flourish is to be attentive. To be attentive is to be loving. And to be loving, attentive, and flourishing is to be *human*."

HOW DO I KNOW WHEN "I'VE MADE IT"?

Ultimately, living like it matters demands love and attention. You have to give the people and things you love focused attention in order to discover this way of living. The goal of this playbook has not been to give you all of the answers, but to draw your attention to parts of your experience that you might otherwise ignore. These are the openings for you to find your own particular way.

In some ways, Gerard Manley Hopkins fits the stereotype of the tortured poet. He struggled with depression, living away from home, a heavy workload, and his poetic calling. He did not have an easy path, but he lived like it mattered. Hopkins invented the term "inscape." "Inscape" describes a set of characteristics that gives each thing its uniqueness and that differentiates it from other things. Hopkins writes about a dead tree, describing its very particular and singular characteristics. The poet is able to see that this tree had markings that no other tree would ever have.

Each of you is marked with "inscape." Finding your "inscape" means escaping the weight of everyone else's expectations for you. It means discovering a wider sense of self, purpose, relationships, and responsibilities. It opens you up to a new horizon, a life that's actually fulfilling, really happy, and truly hopeful. The key is to make sure your life reflects your inscape, your own individual particularities that make you who you are. And to share that inscape with others.

Works Consulted

INTRODUCTION

Jay, Meg. *The Defining Decade: Why Your Twenties Matter and How to Make the Most of Them Now.* New York: Twelve Press. 2013.

CHAPTER ONE

Glickel, Jen. "Dean of Admissions Pleased with Early App Turnout." *The Chicago Maroon*, Nov. 9, 2004, chicagomaroon.com/2015/news/dean-of-admissions-pleased-with-early-app-turnout/.

Markovits, Daniel. *The Meritocracy Trap: How America's Foundational Myth Feeds Inequality, Dismantles the Middle Class, and Devours the Elite.* New York: Penguin Press, 2019.

Jay, Meg. *The Defining Decade.*

Schaeffer, Katherine. "10 Facts about Today's College Graduates." Pew Research Center, April 12, 2022, https://www.pewresearch.org/short-reads/2022/04/12/10-facts-about-todays-college-graduates/.

"University of Chicago." *CollegeAdvisor*, Sept. 17, 2023, www.collegeadvisor.com/colleges/university-of-chicago/.

CHAPTER TWO

Allen, Summer. "Future-Mindedness." *John Templeton Foundation,* Feb. 2019, www.templeton.org/discoveries/future-mindedness.

Badaracco, Joseph. *Defining Moments: When Managers Must Choose Between Right and Right.* Boston: Harvard Business Review Press, 2016, p. 16.

Bauerschmidt, Frederick. *Why the Mystics Matter Now.* Edinburgh: Sorin Books. 2003.

Brooks, David. "How the Bobos Broke America." *The Atlantic,* Sep. 2021, p. 15, https://www.theatlantic.com/magazine/archive/2021/09/blame-the-bobos-creative-class/619492/.

Keillor, Garrison. Interview by Blake Farmer. "Garrison Keillor: Prairie Home Companion Wouldn't Exist without The Ryman." WPLN, May 5, 2017. https://wpln.org/post/garrison-keillor-prairie-home-companion-wouldnt-exist-without-the-ryman/

Sayers, Dorothy. "Why Work?" *Letters to a Diminished Church: Passionate Arguments for the Relevance of Christian Doctrine.* Nashville: Thomas Nelson, 2004, p. 15.

Taylor, Charles. *A Secular Age.* Cambridge, MA: Harvard University Press, 2007.

CHAPTER THREE

American Psychological Association. "Stress in America 2020: A National Mental Health Crisis." 2020, https://www.apa.org/news/press/releases/stress/2020/report-october#:~:text=Nearly%208%20in%2010%20adults,the%20course%20of%20the%20pandemic.

Brueggemann, Walter. *Journey to the Common Good.* Updated edition. Louisville: Westminster John Knox Press, 2021.

Denisen, Isak. "Babette's Feast." *Anecdotes of Destiny and Ehrengard.* New York: Vintage, 1993.

Gerken, Tom. "Video Game Loot Boxes Declared Illegal under Belgium Gambling Laws." BBC News, BBC, Apr. 26, 2018, www.bbc.com/news/technology-43906306.

Goodwin, Renee D., et al. "Trends in Anxiety among Adults in the United States, 2008–2018: Rapid Increases among Young Adults." *Journal of Psychiatric Research* 130 (2020): 441–46, https://doi.org/10.1016/j.jpsychires.2020.08.014.

Harris, Brandonn S., and Jack C. Watson II. "Burnout among Child and Adolescent Athletes." In *Youth Sports in America: The Most Important Issues in Youth Sports Today*, edited by Skye G. Arthur-Banning. Santa Barbara, CA: ABC-CLIO, 2018, pp. 47–58.

Harris, Malcolm. *Kids These Days: Human Capital and the Making of Millennials.* New York: Little Brown and Company, 2017, pp. 20, 83.

Heschel, Abraham Joshua. *The Sabbath: Its Meaning for Modern Man.* New York: Farrar, Straus, and Giroux, 2005, p.18.

Kowert, Rachel, et al. "Social Gaming, Lonely Life? The Impact of Digital Game Play on Adolescents' Social Circles." *Computers in Human Behavior* 36 (2014): 385–90, https://doi.org/10.1016/j.chb.2014.04.003.

Matzkin, Elizabeth, and Kirsten Garvey. "Youth Sports Specialization: Does Practice Make Perfect?" *NASN School Nurse* 34, no. 2 (2019): 100–103, https://doi.org/10.1177/1942602X18814619.

Rainie, Lee, and Andrew Perrin. "Key Findings about Americans' Declining Trust in Government and Each Other." Pew Research Center, Jul. 22, 2019, https://www.pewresearch.org/fact-tank/2019/07/22/key-findings-about-americans-declining- trust-in-government-and-each-other/.

Twenge, Jean M. "The Age of Anxiety: Birth Cohort Change in Anxiety and Neuroticism, 1952–1993." *Journal of Personality and Social Psychology* 79, no. 6 (2000): 1007–1021, https://doi.org/10.1037//0022-3514.79.6.1007.

Twenge, Jean M. *iGen: Why Today's Super-Connected Kids Are Growing Up Less Rebellious, More Tolerant, Less Happy—and Completely Unprepared for Adulthood—and What That Means for the Rest of Us.* New York: Atria Books, 2017.

Witt, Peter A., and Tek B. Dangi. "Why Children/Youth Drop Out of Sports." *Journal of Park and Recreation Administration* 36, no. 3 (2018): 191–99, https://doi.org/10.18666/JPRA-2018-V36-I3-8618.

CHAPTER FOUR

Csíkszentmihályi, Mihály. *Flow: The Psychology of Optimal Experience*. New York: Harper Perennial Modern Classics, 2008.

Kowert, Rachel, et al. "Social Gaming, Lonely Life?"

Shakya, Holly B., and Nicholas A. Christakis. "Association of Facebook Use with Compromised Well-Being: A Longitudinal Study." *American Journal of Epidemiology* 185, no. 3 (2017): 203–11, https://doi.org/10.1093/aje/kww189.

Twenge, Jean M., et al. "Less In-Person Social Interaction with Peers among U.S. Adolescents in the 21st Century and Links to Loneliness." *Journal of Social and Personal Relationships* 36, no. 6 (2019): 1892–1913, https://doi.org/10.1177/0265407519836170.

CHAPTER FIVE

Baldwin, James. *The Fire Next Time*. New York: Vintage, 1992, p. 40.

Damour, Lisa. "Why Teenagers Mix Drinking and Sex." *New York Times*, Nov. 14, 2018. https://www.nytimes.com/2018/11/14/well/family/why-teenagers-mix-drinking-and- sex.html.

Finnegan, Mary. "Bad Men and Other Women: A Riveting Case Study on the Sordid Cocktail of Sex, Alcohol, and the Dorm Room." *Digital Library@ Villanova University*, 2015, https://digital.library.villanova.edu/Item/vudl:456798.

Harris, Malcolm. *Kids These Days*, p. 188.

Hattersley-Gray, Robin. "The Sexual Assault Statistics Everyone Should Know." *Campus Safety*, Mar. 5, 2018, https://www.campussafetymagazine.com/safety/sexual-assault-statistics-and-myths/.

Herbenick, Debby, et al. "The Alcohol Contexts of Consent, Wanted Sex, Sexual Pleasure, and Sexual Assault: Results from a Probability Survey of Undergraduate Students." *Journal of American College Health* 67, no. 2 (2019): 114–52, https://doi.org/10.1080/07448481.2018.1462827.

New, Michael J. "New CDC Data Show Continued Declines in Teen Sexual Activity." *National Review*, Feb. 15, 2023, www.nationalreview.com/corner/new-cdc-data-show-continued-declines-in-teen-sexual-activity/#:~:text=Between%202019%20and%202021%2C%20the,decline%20of%20eight%20percentage%20points.

Weissbourd, Richard, et al. "The Talk: How Adults Can Promote Young People's Healthy Relationships and Prevent Misogyny and Sexual Harassment." *Making Caring Project at Harvard Graduate School of Education*, 2018, p. 9, https://static1.squarespace.com/static/5b7c56e255b02c683659fe43/t/5bd51a 0324a69425bd079b59/1540692500558/mcc_the_talk_final.pdf.

Wilman, Christian. *My Bright Abyss: Meditation of a Modern Believer.* New York: Farrar, Straus, and Giroux, 2013.

CHAPTER SIX

Lewis, C. S. *The Four Loves.* Harvest Books, 1971.

Parker, Kim, and Renee Stepler. "As US Marriage Rate Hovers at 50%, Education Gap in Marital Status Widens." *Pew Research Center*, Sep. 14, 2017, https://www.pewresearch.org/fact-tank/2017/09/14/ as-u-s-marriage-rate-hovers-at-50-education-gap-in-marital-status-widens/.

Wallace, David Foster. "This Is Water." Kenyon College Commencement, May 21, 2005, Kenyon College, Gambier, OH. Address. https://fs.blog/2012/04/ david-foster-wallace-this-is-water/.

Wang, Wendy. "The Link between a College Education and a Lasting Marriage." Pew Research Center, Dec. 4, 2015, https://www.pewresearch.org/ fact-tank/2015/12/04/education-and-marriage/.

Wilman, Christian. *My Bright Abyss: Meditation of a Modern Believer.*

CONCLUSION

O'Donohue, John. *To Bless the Space between Us.* New York: Doubleday, 2008.

Higgins, Lesley, ed. *The Collected Works of Gerard Manley Hopkins. Vol. III: Diaries, Journals and Notebooks.* Oxford: Oxford University Press, 2015.

Hopkins, Gerard Manley. *The Journals and Papers of Gerard Manley Hopkins.* Oxford: Oxford University Press, 1959.

JOURNAL

JOURNAL